T0274847

Praise for *The Molino*

"Melani 'Mele' Martinez provides an in-depth look into the daily workings of El Rapido, a once-celebrated Tucson restaurant known for making the best tamales. Through heartfelt essays and *pensamientos*, Martinez's portrayal of how it took a village to sustain the molino, which, in turn, nourished the community, is both captivating and enlightening. I highly recommend this informative and beautifully written book."

—Lydia R. Otero, author of *In the Shadows of the Freeway: Growing Up Brown and Queer*

"Melani Martinez's sumptuous words sizzled in my gut! *The Molino* is a feast, a gripping story about food, family, and ghosts that doubles as a microhistory of downtown Tucson. Martinez's lyrical prose will keep you coming back to taste—and learn—more and more."

—Daniel José Camacho, writer and former editor at Fortress Press and *Sojourners*

"A powerful, visceral, and sometimes bitter and humorous memoir of heritage, identity, assimilation, and loss through gentrification."

—Patricia Preciado Martin, author of *El Milagro and Other Stories*

"Melani Martinez's poetic vignettes about life inside her father's molino business are so palpable, you can almost feel the volcanic stone. But what really captivates is her gentle rumination on what it means to be home, the forces that shape us, and the ghostly memories that we can't shake, no matter how hard we try."

—Lesley Téllez, author of *Eat Mexico*

"Martinez's words provide a sensorial history and a vivid portal into Tucson's Mexican past and present. The desert imagery and the warmth and grit of the kitchen shape every page. These precious and intimate family stories beautifully capture the memories and imagination of a Tucson daughter."

—Michelle Téllez, author of *Border Women and the Community of Maclovio Rojas*

"Astonishingly gorgeous and one of the best books I've read in a long time. Melani Martinez combines storytelling and lyricism with such power and precision, *The Molino* becomes an urgent page-turner, a work that transforms haunt, loss, and elegy into the wisdom of the seer, the self-proclaimed knowledge of being, and of having been, a tamalero's daughter. This is as much a familial history as it is of neighborhoods in downtown Tucson, where poverty and gentrification intersect to reveal that grinding labor can never overcome the consuming demands of inexhaustible hunger, where sacrifice and luck buy little against death and sorrow, where house and home are lost to social factories that erase thought, dreams, and the possibility of sleep—but where the telling results in the triumph of the teller who, in love, raises her own true spirit while laying phantoms to rest."

—Gina Franco, author of *The Accidental*

"Step into the enchanted world of Martinez's evocative prose and poetry, where the aroma of freshly made tamales spins a tale of love and a familial legacy within Tucson's El Presidio neighborhood. Martinez intricately crafts a vibrant portrayal of a family deeply entrenched in tradition, their lives interwoven with the vibrant tapestry of Barrio Menlo's streets. Martinez's book has a level of intimacy previously unavailable to others, yet she delivers an unfiltered view into familial history, capturing 'remembering as an anchor in an ocean,' from Nana's whispered tales to Tata's enduring presence. These haunting vignettes shape a moving coming-of-age story, guiding a young Mexican woman on a journey of self-discovery that honors the heartfelt communion of shared feasts and the resilience of family bonds."

—Diana Marie Delgado, editor of *Like a Hammer Across the Page: Poets Writing Against Mass Incarceration*

THE MOLINO

MELANI MARTINEZ

THE UNIVERSITY OF
ARIZONA PRESS

TUCSON

The University of Arizona Press
www.uapress.arizona.edu

We respectfully acknowledge the University of Arizona is on the land and territories of Indigenous peoples. Today, Arizona is home to twenty-two federally recognized tribes, with Tucson
being home to the O'odham and the Yaqui. Committed to diversity and inclusion, the University
strives to build sustainable relationships with sovereign Native Nations and Indigenous commu-
nities through education offerings, partnerships, and community service.

ISBN-13: 978-0-8165-5261-0 (hardcover)
ISBN-13: 978-0-8165-5262-7 (ebook)

Cover design by Leigh McDonald
Cover photograph adapted from author's personal photo
Designed and typeset by Leigh McDonald in Bell MT Std 10.5/14, Hardwick WF, and Payson
WF (display)

Publication of this book is made possible in part by the proceeds of a permanent endowment created with the assistance of a Challenge Grant from the National Endowment for the Humanities,
a federal agency.

Library of Congress Cataloging-in-Publication Data
Names: Martinez, Melani, 1977– author.
Title: The molino : a memoir / Melani Martinez.
Description: Tucson : University of Arizona Press, [2024]
Identifiers: LCCN 2023048396 (print) | LCCN 2023048397 (ebook) | ISBN 9780816552610
    (hardcover) | ISBN 9780816552627 (ebook)
Subjects: LCSH: Martinez, Melani, 1977– | Martínez family. | Mexican Americans—Arizona—
    Tucson—Biography. | Food habits—Arizona—Tucson. | Tucson (Ariz.)—History—20th
    century. | LCGFT: Autobiographies.
Classification: LCC F819.T99 M553 2024 (print) | LCC F819.T99 (ebook) | DDC
    979.1/7760046872073092 [B]—dc23/eng/20231214
LC record available at https://lccn.loc.gov/2023048396
LC ebook record available at https://lccn.loc.gov/2023048397

Printed in the United States of America
♾ This paper meets the requirements of ANSI/NISO Z39.48-1992 (Permanence of Paper).

This book is dedicated to
my brother, who is always beside me,
my mother, who is the keeper of secrets,
and my father, the tamalero champion of the world.

CONTENTS

PART III

PART IV

PART V

PART VI

PART VII

ACKNOWLEDGMENTS

I am grateful to my Goucher College mentors, Diana Hume George, Leslie Rubinkowski, Tom French, and Suzannah Lessard, for their patient guidance so many years ago as I started this manuscript.

My sincerest gratitude to *Fourth Genre* for selecting one of the earliest Molino essays as the winner of the publication's 2004 Editors' Prize. That recognition was pivotal for me as a writer and helped motivate me to complete the manuscript. Also, many thanks to the Arizona Commission on the Arts, the Arts Foundation for Tucson and Southern Arizona, and the Tucson Festival of Books for providing opportunities for us Tucson writers.

A special thanks to Diza Sauers, Alison Deming, Lydia Otero, Norma Cantú, Sarah Cortez, Lisa Ohlen Harris, Gina Franco, Logan Phillips, Sara Hubbs, and Kimi Eielse for your empowering instruction, modeling, and mentorship. Thank you to all the members of Escritorx, especially Charlie Buck, Estella Gonzalez, Monique Soria, and Lesley Téllez, for providing a compassionate writing community. Thank you also to Alex Jimenez for your artistry in creating illustrated maps of Tucson for this work.

To my dad's family, especially Tío Tito, Tías Susie and Yvette, and my cousin Martin, thank you for all the memories you have shared. I could not have done this work without you.

Finally, thank you to my husband, Jason, and my daughters, Lola and Gloria, for your extraordinary patience and understanding. I love you so much.

THE MOLINO

prologue

do not be afraid
I am no sleepy mexican
I am not asleep
but I am

a patient
thought cloud
above a mud plaster
well of water I know

rest
I am the sun
quake cracking adobe

I am the word
I am home

I am waiting
on a presidio wall
waiting for my apple
my little girl
mijita

—*el pensamiento*

PART I

Corn Sister

I know the smell of corn like a little sister sleeping beside me, wearing my clothes, and stealing my hairbrush. I can smell her on my fingers. She's in the air along the highway. She is on my tongue. She is the color of cream, a perfume that fills my father's kitchen. She will be ground, spread, and steamed with manteca and chile. She will hold my hands and walk down to the river with me. She will grow old with me.

The Molino

The molino has a motor song, like a train, reaching out beyond the road, the river, and the mountain. The molino is my father's machine, and it sits in the back of the room. It is bigger than a refrigerator. It is bigger than a year. It is bigger than the moving truck that will come someday to haul it away. Beneath a burning cloud there is a grinding stone where the molino eats corn and perhaps misbehaved children. A molino swallows and changes things. It prepares bodies for the rest that will come. Its work is never done. The molino is like my father, a mechanical parent, hard at work pushing and shoving the meat out of little kernels of corn.

This is my father's kitchen, a place for changing, a way to use every drop. In this kitchen, nothing goes down the drain. There is no falling to the floor. Nothing is left behind. This kitchen does not wait on you. It doesn't hold its breath at depressions or recessions, nor at openings and closings. It is perpetual fire and water. My family calls this place, this heat and steam, this tamal and tortilla factory, the Molino. Everybody on the outside calls it El Rapido, a lunch counter, a place to get in line for a red chile burrito or a dozen tamales. It is a place for high-noon quesadillas and cinnamon tea over crushed ice. It is a place that means salt and chile and lime. And it means what it says. And to us it says, *I am the grinder.*

The grinder's days are numbered, like the glossy-paper calendars ordered from a man in México who pretends to love my father. They are customized to read "El Rapido—Meet and Eat." They are rolled, rubber-banded, and packed in bags with Christmas tamales for our customers to unfold later, to mark the days with pictures of Popo and Itza: eternal, volcanic love. "Food you'll remember," my father's calendars read, for January through December.

Many people come to work in my father's kitchen. Girls in aprons scramble here, looking for their life in corn. Boys build some muscle. Cooks, food preppers, and money changers fuss over shredded cheese and chile and watch the bills pile up on the mixer. We stay a long time. We won't leave until every drop is drawn out, settled in the veins, until the sun sets on this long workday.

I can see my father praying and stirring.

Everybody around here knows my father, Tony Peyron. They know him by the sound of his voice shouting over the deli case and by his hands reaching into the pockets of a blue apron. I watch him stir a lime-ash-covered caldron of boiling nixtamal with an oar, like a fisherman in a sinking boat. Someday I will wish that he could walk on water. I will wish for many things watching him at the mill, watching the crushing, the volcanic stones pushing against each other inside the molino. I will watch until they close the door.

FIGURE 1 Tony Peyron with his sisters, Susie and Yvette in front of El Rapido in the early 1980s. Photo by David Burckhalter from author's personal collection."

my apples

have you seen
the girls
their eyes and bellies like giant apples
their hair like clay-covered string
broke joke penny loafer seams
unraveling backpack and
sweat back elbow
grease work
smelling like me
like oregano leaves
like ajo

I see
mijita
I am
the one who sees

—*el pensamiento*

77 West Washington / 220 North Meyer

My father's kitchen used to be a car garage. It sits next to the building where my nana Juanita grew up, a Sonoran-style house with a pyramid roof in the historic Presidio neighborhood of downtown Tucson. At the corner of Washington Street and Meyer Avenue, the property has two addresses, and my family occupied both for fifty years before I began working in my father's kitchen.

FIGURE 2 Tony Peyron on the corner of Washington Street and Meyer Avenue in the late 1940s. Photo from author's personal collection.

———————

The garage kitchen faces Washington opposite Old Town Artisans, a set of row houses, around a large courtyard, that used to be apartments in the early 1900s—all converted to retail shops selling art, southwestern jewelry, and souvenirs to tourists. When she married and left the house on Meyer, my nana Juanita moved across the street to live in a one-room apartment at Old Town for a few years with my tata Alberto and their first two babies, my uncle Alberto (Tito) and my father, Antonio (Tony). Both babies had been born a few steps away at a maternity ward called the Stork's Nest at 223 North Court Avenue. My nana Juanita never returned to live in her father's house, but she continued to work for him, and eventually opened a beauty shop in the northern room of the old house that had its own front door also facing Meyer. My father says the house and the beauty salon faced Jeff's Chinese Market in those days, but by the time I was born, Jeff moved his market to Barrio Menlo, leaving nothing across the street except a parking lot for lawyers and the setting sun. Eventually, the house and beauty salon became anonymous, then invisible, to people passing by. For decades, nothing marked this site as significant, and if anyone cared to wonder what it was like inside these structures, they probably assumed the whole place was abandoned. But it wasn't vacant. Not really.

Between the house on Meyer and the garage kitchen on Washington, small, clear plastic bags of water hang from the wood-beam ceiling to keep the flies away, and an uneven brick path opens to a tiny patio, where I stand when I want to watch the rain. I can't see rain through the kitchen's windows, opaque with grease and steam. Most of the windows are broken in the old house at North Meyer Street, but in the right sunset light, you can just make out the paled words my great-grandfather painted on the original storefront window: "GROCERY / EL RÁPIDO MOLINO / De Nixtamal / Manufactura De Tortillas Y Masa." This sun-bleached inscription, this emblem, lingers unnoticed like a ghost on the sidewalk, with only a few desert weeds poking through cement to keep it company.

Briny mud walls hold up the pyramidal roof of the old house where the piping is exposed and the plumbing reeks. In the kitchen, the ceiling is high enough to fit industrial-height refrigerators that hum twenty-four hours a day. There are six-burner stoves lighting a fierce fire each morning. There are two sinks almost big enough for baths. On the east end, a grill is set beside warming tables and a deli case. Stainless steel reflects fluorescent light from wall to wall. The cash register is hidden behind swinging wood-slat doors, the kind I've only seen in Bugs Bunny cartoons and Westerns.

This part of downtown is probably forgotten by most of the city of Tucson. Field trip students visit the Tucson Museum of Art a block away, and snowbirds stroll through Old Town Artisans across the street, but only a couple dozen people still live on this street, and most of the locals who spend time here in historic adobes, mansions, and duplexes are just here from nine to five. My great-grandfather Aurelio Perez was the first to open El Rapido in this house in 1933. He made tortillas and tamales and sold them to the people in the neighborhood. He sold chile, fresh cheese, cigarettes, and groceries. He ground people's corn for them, prepared their masa in the molino. He took phone orders and walked door to door peddling panocha and oregano. Like my father later, my great-grandfather Aurelio employed his family as much as he could. His daughters, my nana Juanita and all her seven sisters, worked there on and off to help make food and profit. Even after some were married, after children, after the war and after women's liberation, even after their husbands died.

My great-aunt Soledad Perez, Aurelio's oldest daughter, took over the business in the 1950s. She was one of the only women running a business in Tucson at the time. She was a beautiful choir singer, single, strong, trailblazing, and clever. She was sixty-two years old when she finally married, but no one has told me her love story. Maybe no one knows it. I've been told stories about her wedding day, November 9, 1976, a gorgeous Friday afternoon in the Old Pueblo. It was extraordinary that Soledad would stop working, that the Molino would stop running, but she closed El Rapido for a whole week to celebrate the occasion. It was so rare for the Molino to be closed, there was even an announcement in the *Arizona Daily Star.*

My father and his siblings recall how amazing that day was, like everyone was high on life—dancing, drinking, smoking, shouting. That was the day my father told my mother, only a few months before their own wedding, that Soledad was his favorite

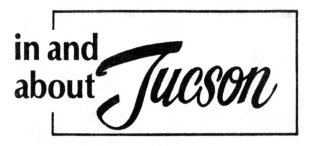

By EDITH SAYRE ARMSTRONG

Closed For Wedding

El Rapido has been closed and you may have wondered why. Proprietress Soledad Perez found it necessary to shut down the tortilla factory for a few days to prepare for her wedding Friday to Dolores Tarazon. The couple was married at St. Augustine's Cathedral.

Patrons will be happy to know that it'll soon be business as usual at El Rapido, but with the added attraction of Mr. Tarazon, who, by the way, plans to add chorizo to the menu.

FIGURE 3 Edith Sayre Armstrong for the *Arizona Daily Star,* Sunday, November 14, 1976.

aunt. Soledad wore her hair in a permanent, dyed dark brown. She walked down the aisle of St. Augustine's Cathedral. Mr. Dolores S. Tarazon, a widower with three children, was her groom. But Soledad was not retiring to become a housewife. Instead, Mr. Tarazon, as he is called by everyone in my family, had plans to help Soledad expand the menu and to make the Molino a real lunch counter.

Soledad knew one day she'd have to part with the work, that she'd need to spend more time at the home of Mr. Tarazon than at 77 West Washington. Less than three years after their wedding, Mr. Tarazon passed away, and Soledad was left alone again in the Molino's kitchen. I can imagine her folding and stirring and wrapping food up with grief. I can imagine her invisible movements by the fire. And I have visions of her being comforted by ollas, the steaming tamal pots, that sat scorched and misshapen on the wire shelves, huddling together beside her like a family of bereaved misfits.

That is when my aunt Yvette, my father's youngest sister, suggested that Tony would be the perfect person to run it for the family, because he had been so close with his grandfather Aurelio and because he had such an incredible work ethic. My father wasn't just a hard worker. He was a beast, Yvette said. He had the perfect temperament for a Molino. Soledad agreed. Not long after my brother, Ricky, was born, Soledad stopped coming to the Molino all together, and my father took charge of the kitchen and incorporated the business. My mother suggested he name the business after the kids, so on paper he titled it the Melrick Corporation.

I begin working for my father as soon as I can walk, talk, and take orders. Alongside my tía Micaela, my first task is to help make corn tortillas. Tía Mica feeds masa balls into a giant black machine lined with gas burners, and I stand on the other end of the conveyor belt to lift the toasty rounds off the belt and into a

stack that can be bagged. This is my introduction to burned fingertips. Mica insists each tortilla be stacked evenly. I pile circular
columns of tortillas up like a smoking tower. Mica is frail and thin,
moving slowly, but she stands close to me. She never looks me in
the eyes, but she watches over me.

Before long, my little brother shares in the work beside me. He
is named Richard after my father's cousin, a World War II hero
who died in combat, but we all call him Ricky. I get the big jobs
in the kitchen and Ricky, eighteen and a half months younger
than I am, follows right behind, his dimples flashing regularly at
customers. Together we spend summers and weekends and school
vacation days in my father's kitchen. Smothered in Tucson summer sweat, we discuss the summer movies we want to see, the
air-conditioned theaters we want to visit. We pace the floor of this
old garage dreaming of school days as the bottom of our tennis
shoes stick to the grime. It seems everything in the kitchen is
filmed with yesterday's fat, which no amount of soap can loosen.
It is hot, it is humid, and for us it is hell. Even my father hates it
sometimes. Still, he will put to work any child who asks for it. I
imagine every child on the block is subject to his kitchen if my
father catches them idle. My brother's soccer teammates, people
off the street, poor friends, poor family, people itching for something to do—they all find work here. They come in looking for
minimum wage, or just below, and find it from my father, who is
both generous and greedy all in the same paycheck. They shred
cheese, slice chiles, wash dishes, spread masa, sweep, steal, trade,
and keep my father company. He loves them and uses them. He
lets nothing go to waste.

My father sells food with no labels and no special packaging.
There is no list of ingredients. He uses what he has. Rules are
ignored, corners cut through. As long as the inspector is satisfied,
my father doesn't need a fancy menu or personalized salsa packets.
His food is more than enough; his recipes are old, but these are the
kinds of meals that shoot arrows through you.

Everything in my father's kitchen seems to live forever. It will never be a modern kitchen, but once in a while a new appliance or object is added that inches it further away from the Depression era. There is a microwave, a huge mirror engraved with the image of Selena Quintanilla on the wall, and a University of Arizona Wildcat football itinerary taped anywhere it will stick. There are papers with scribbled notes clinging to the plaster walls my father paints and repaints bright white. The swamp cooler serves no real purpose. The tilting ceiling fan in the front room hovers over the heads of customers and will never fall, but the fear is there. My father will fix anything and everything with a piece of string or a strip of tape. He will keep up on his rent checks, paid on time to the tías, my nana Juanita's sisters, who own the property. And everything will work.

I suppose the buildings, like him, have not changed much over the years, even though age creeps up on both, threatening destruction like a big yellow bulldozer. One thing stays the same: the molino, the grinder.

I watch my father hunch over the mouth of the molino, pushing corn down its throat. I watch the corn change to mush and slide out the bottom. It is loud, as though it is angry, vibrating back and forth with intensity. The molino's engine is covered with a black slickness that smells of smoke. A combination of dirt and grease. A grime impenetrable. It is not really a monster, I know, but I can feel it breathing like a hungry animal. I wonder how people can ignore it when they walk into the kitchen, as if it is a mural on the wall or an extension of the underground piping system. I wonder why they never mention it. It demands my full attention. I know it is the most important thing to my father, the most valuable of the never-ending tools. Its motor has been replaced several times, but my father has great faith in its abilities. He memorizes the phone number for the repairman who must come from Mexico or Los Angeles to service the machine. But it won't break down. It can't stop. The molino and my father won't stop grinding.

I will find myself in this kitchen even when my father has hired new workers to replace me. Sometimes I will need the money. Sometimes I need a place to go, even if I don't belong there. I hate it most of the time. The chile stings. Hot pot vapors flash-steam burns on my arms and face. I itch all over with corn silk. My father never grows tired repeating the same messages to me: *Don't waste. Spread thin. Move quick.* I learn to shudder at the sound of a cowbell hanging from the front door. I begin to judge everyone here, their lack of class. I resent my inability to communicate with anyone. I hate my father's broken briefcase splattered with dry specks of masa. I will call him a tyrant. I will hate not having a word to call myself. It will feel like a waste of time. At some point, I begin to hate all my father's energy spent in the kitchen. Nothing left over. No investments, nothing to show. Just work. By the time I know all this, my brother will be gone. My mother too. Only my father will keep the stones grinding until they grind themselves.

I am the girl with brown eyes and hair like clay-covered string. I am the girl in broken penny loafers. Sweaty back, dusty elbows. I was born in this kitchen, inside the Molino, and I am a stranger in the middle of cream and corn and charred skin.

vapor, vapor

remember your Creator
before cob bottom before
emptiness comes
coming

to cover the light sun moon and stars
to bring rain where it was already flooding

before the housekeepers shudder
and toe tip to hip
backbones bow down

don't wait for grinders
to cease dining doors
shut to the streets remember before
the sound of stones slick and cool and mum
is the hum of the machine
but the birds
keep you from sleep and a gray part
fear part frailty cuts all warm longings and olives
and books in half or less

before all the daughters of music
your song voice
quiet
I will help you
remember me

—*el pensamiento*

The Sleepy Mexican

The sounds of Ramón Ayala's accordion strike out like electric sparks from a chrome boom box blasting inside the Molino. *Voy a buscar*, he cries, *un rinconcito en el cielo!* His voice reminds me of one of my father's friends calling on the telephone, that boom on the other end of the line. I string the sounds together in my head; between my English and Ayala's Spanish is a reedy accordion moan, an organ quiver that shakes the kitchen and speaks every tongue. This is the sound of Sundays. Ayala's accordion carries the Molino out of a Tuesday or Wednesday. Not even a celebratory Friday afternoon can compete with his melodeon. When we hear *y cuando caiga la noche te daré mi amor*, my father will crank the volume to 10 on the boom box and only hear Sunday.

The sound blasts out of the Molino and onto the sidewalk where my uncle Tito squints in the sun. Hidden under denim jeans and Workmens boots, his pinched legs and twisted feet climb a step stool. He looks down at his bucket of paint and makes swirls in the acrylic. His back is strong. With each careful step, he adjusts his weight and his long braids of black and gray drift back and forth, like two legs with equal gait. On his forehead, a bandana tied in a neat knot catches the drops of sweat that roll from the crown of his head down toward his ears. His eyes squint in blinding sunlight, but his mind's eye is open to the study, the image my father has asked him to paint on the storefront: a little man, asleep.

The man's head is bowed, and his face hidden below a hat. His hands are crossed, resting on a round belly. His feet are bare and his back leans on a blossoming saguaro. The image of this little man sleeping is two-dimensional, several shades of brown, and permanently stamped in the upper left-hand corner of an old receipt book that belonged to Tito's grandfather Aurelio. This little man is my uncle Tito's mural model, painted under the words "El Rapido Mexican Food."

The man's belly swells with Tito's brush and the sound of Ayala singing, *¡Voy a buscar!* Tito paints him short and fat, resting under the words that hang in his sky. Wrapped in a shout of *un rinconcito en el cielo*, the resting man is silent on the wall. *You know, he makes me dream of México*, Tito tells me. But I don't think he means Mexico today. He must mean an older version, a Mexico like in the movies; a place where people stop, close shop, and rest; a place where turning off and leaning or lying down in the shade is a respectful act. The way Tito talks, I want to go there, where dreams are allowed in the middle of the workday while the sun still sits high in the sky. A whole country made up of siestas, can you imagine? *Para llevar a mi amor.*

Mr. Cota-Robles is the first to protest Tito's painting of the little sleeping man. Cota-Robles's law office is on Meyer Avenue and when he turns the corner to see Tito's mural, he stops to discuss why this is a mistake.

It's no good, he says. *You know, this thing makes us look stupid. And lazy.*

Tito is unsure how to react and doesn't respond. He doesn't have the chance to be upset by Mr. Cota-Robles's comments until after the lawyer has walked away, when he begins to think and gather his paint and brushes. The lawyer's words seem to hang there by the storefront, flapping in the breeze like the fringe at the edge of the little sleeping man's blanket.

My father does not understand the critique either. After Mr. Cota-Robles leaves, my father says, *I don't understand what the hell he is talking about. Why say that? That guy said it makes Mexicans look lazy! What?* he holds out his left hand like a target, like go ahead and shoot me. *I mean, come on. That was my grandfather's logo! That's the El Rapido Man, you know what I mean? What's wrong with it?*

I nod my head in agreement, *Right*, I say, not knowing how else to talk about it.

Hey man, he's ours! my father says stirring the pot and sucking the air like he's taking a drag.

I never wonder who the Sleepy Mexican is. I don't look at him when I walk out of the Molino. I don't want to look at him. I don't want to see short and fat, asleep. I don't see a face hidden under a sombrero, and I don't consider his prayer hands on a belly, nor thorns in his neck. When I think of him, I think of grinding. It is the same feeling I have when the desert sun hammers down on my head. Grinding. When I hear an accordion, I think of grinding and grinding. Each year the boom box blasts new tunes in the Molino, but Ayala is always there ringing in my ears: *Voy a buscar un rinconcito en el cielo, para escondernos tú y yo.* The words are lost on me. The Sleepy Mexican means nothing but work. Work that you don't want to do for the rest of your life even though it is one of the few things in the world that makes you feel like you might actually be home.

None of us in my father's kitchen have heard the name Sleepy Mexican before, and so we stop talking about things we don't understand. Tito climbs the step stool again and again to touch up his mural on the Molino. The sleeping man fades for a while, then comes back to life with Tito's brush dipped in bright greens and blues. Other people come to my father and complain about the sleeping man, but he waves his hands at them, only pretends to hear them, or laughs like trickling water. I begin to forget the sleeping man is even there. Most everyone else ignores him too. He may draw some close enough to touch his clothes or run their hand over his stucco saguaro. But some are angered. They detest him. His name makes the flies scatter.

Tito tells me that he has decided to add something special to the mural, a revision to his artistic vision, a layer that no one will protest. He paints two little yellow eyes inside the dark hole of the sleeping man's saguaro. *Like the eyes of an owl,* Tito tells me. And the eyes never close, not even on Sundays.

PART II

Ghost, Part 1

In the warm water, the corn husks softened. I scooped masa and chile onto ojas, one by one. I remember spoons, cold pork stained chile red, bowls of green olives and raisins, and icy, raw fingers until maybe a hundred dozen tamales were done. It was almost Christmas, but there was no end in sight to the tamales, piling up in the refrigerator and the freezer and the tabletops and the stoves, piled on the mixer, in the deli case, even on the molino. Tamales were everywhere my eyes landed. I daydreamed there in the crowd of them. In my father's kitchen, I felt tossed and turned. I waded through waves of tamales. Their rhythm sometimes rocked me into other places where I was no longer a girl in an apron, places that were not Tucson. Sometimes, while my hands worked, I landed on a beach far away from the Presidio. I climbed a cliff's edge and sat with the sunset, my hands clean, my breath up and down with the waves. I'd dream and plan. I'd leave the Molino for real and begin a new life where I could be someone else, where I could dance.

Go take those tamales to the freezer! my father shouted, his words like splashes of ice water on my face. *And bring back some ojas*, he said without looking up from his hands in the mixer. The freezer and bags of ojas were stored in the house next to the Molino. The old house was a good escape.

When my father wasn't looking or paying attention, I would slide my hands along the cool plaster walls of that old house. The floor was the oldest floor I had ever walked on, its patina created over years of shoe soles brushing along. No one was living in the house, but it was still partially furnished. Everything there rested in a shadow. The light switches didn't work, and the windows were nearly blacked out with grit or dusty curtains. On the east side of the house, the floor descended into a sunken room where my father stored his food supplies. There, a lightbulb hung from the center of the ceiling by a long, thin string that I could barely reach even when I was fully grown. The room had a window to Washington Street, but it was covered with dirt on the outside and venetian blinds thick with dust on the inside. Nothing was visible when you looked out the window, and it let in little light. This storage room was packed with fifty-pound bags of rice and beans. The walls were lined with metal shelves, where my father kept large canisters of spices, 109-ounce cans of tomato puree, and packages of plastic and Styrofoam containers. There were bales of ojas piled to tall ceilings and deep chest freezers filled with shredded beef or pork. The rest of the house held other items that belonged to someone else, but I wasn't sure to whom. There were no explicit owners of anything there, just a place to hold every-thing that no one could bear to throw away. I convinced myself once that the contents of that home belonged to me, at least in part, and I took items for myself that I thought no one would miss: a tiny strip of fabric with iridescent beads sewn on, a moth-eaten housedress that hung in the armoire.

Each small room of the house was cluttered. Boxes covered most of the floor in the bedrooms and even more boxes barricaded the room that was my grandmother's old beauty salon—a tiny room with its storefront on Meyer Avenue. There were heavy curtains hanging in the front room. The built-in bookcase still held books and framed photos to stare at and reach for in the dark. There were men's ties hung on wire hangers in an armoire. There were religious relics, plastic rosaries, and knickknacks in jewelry boxes. In the tiny kitchen, there was a wooden spoon lying on an old stove, and a cupboard kept a half-full saltshaker. In thick layers of dust, I wrote my name or drew faces. My fingerprints were on almost everything in that old house. The things I couldn't get my hands on were hanging high on the walls or up in the attic. Many times, I stood in the zaguan and pushed the buttons on the old broken floor tube radio, then gazed at the tobacco store wall plaques, hung in the zaguan. These chalkware faces were brown and flanked with red-and-blue feather headdresses. The whites of their eyes caught my attention and stared back at me. I remember they faced each other, only a couple feet apart up on the wall. I tested them in the shadows of the zaguan, watching as long as I could to make sure those eyes didn't move like the eyes of elaborate paintings or statues in scary stories. The eyes seemed to watch over the house, guarding whatever was there.

The relics abiding in that old house were the only family portrait I could see over and over again, the only way to picture my ancestors before I was born. I was curious but also scared of the old house. It was a faded photo of the unknown. I knew spoons and masa and chile and my father's kitchen well, but I didn't know many other images or stories of my family. I'm not sure if my father comprehended my fear and fascination with the old, dead things I was sure were living there in the floorboards. He never explained much of anything to me, and in school I was taught no history lessons that told this story, no definitions of these Presidio spirits, who they were, how they lived, ate, and died. I had been given the incidental details, anecdotes of legends, the one-minute folklore that was my family, but I never knew the full stories. I hadn't yet learned that all that had been lost, all that was now sleeping quietly, would die again, and again.

I carried a plastic bin of tamales from the kitchen, through the patio, and into the old house. Plopping the bin down, I hovered in the doorway of the freezer for a moment, exhaling slowly to watch my breath form clouds in the chilled air. I walked into the lower room, where there was enough light to see large objects resting on shelves: chafing dishes, plastic bins, large gunnysacks. I jumped up to reach the string to the lightbulb hanging from the center of the ceiling, where it swung back and forth taunting me. On a second or third try, my fingertips clamped around it and I pulled hard. But there was no light, and in the darkness, I suddenly heard a loud noise in the house that made me flinch. It was not a thud or a thunder. Not a pierce or high-pitched sound from a stray cat. It was not scurrying feet nor pounding feet. But the sound was felt—and the feeling seemed to come from beneath the floor. It was a walking or dragging or dropping. I wondered later if I had actually heard it, but that question made me feel crazy because I knew I had. It wasn't a daydream. It was not my imagination. I know it was real because I struggled to process it for the moment after I heard it, the moment that I felt a fear I rarely experienced as a child outside of feverish nightmares. These racing thoughts were replaced with just one message: *Get out, get out now.*

I flung the door open to enter my father's kitchen and stood there silently.

Where are my ojas? my father asked.

I heard a noise, I said. *In the house.*

Go get the ojas! And bring back some lids for the salsa cups too, he barked. *Start chopping those onions and pick up that thing on the floor. Get me my ojas! Immediately, if not sooner!*

I'm not going back in there, I said, shaking my head.

in the mirror dimly

you call me pancho my name is holy

I have lived in your house
cramped on your shelves
since christmas

I am
in the mirror with you each morning
you wander
blanket-drunk joints
relic bones like butter
fall on glass and metal
to reconcile self and self

but I am
the one considering your nose scar your collarbone skin tag
sinuous left earlobe I have met you
over and over

under straw hat tucked
kneecaps wrapped in quarried zarape
who do you say that I am
a vampire to you

in the mirror dimly
dotted palms and double chin

there
I am that I am
haunting your everyday
reflections with a sabbath promise
face to face

—*el pensamiento*

Juanita's Beauty

Around the corner from the Molino, Juanita's Beauty Shop sat vacant and locked. On its steps, Ricky and I watched rainbows appear at the end of monsoon rains; we drank root beer and ate quesadillas as we listened to the call of white-winged doves. Now and then we'd try to look in the painted windows of the salon, but we couldn't see what was inside, all that my nana had worked for. Long before any of us were born, Nana went to beauty school. This was her way out of the Molino, a chance to be her own, to color, curl, and comb herself something beautiful. Before she married Alberto, before her children, Tito, Tony, Susie, and Yvette, were born, she learned to clip hair and give permanents. She brewed chemicals. She collected hairpins in glass jars and hairnets in paper envelopes. She stared into the mirror, on her feet, making waves. Each day, she boldly walked away from the Molino, five or six blocks away, and entered the beauty college on East Congress Street. On the way, she caught Alberto's eye.

Juanita's Beauty Shop was connected to the house on Meyer, but the door to its room was locked. When Ricky and I played in the zaguan, racing up and down the long hallway, I'd often stop to test the door, but I could never turn the nob. I imagined a glossy vinyl floor in geometric patterns, a long line of tall, mint-colored hair dryers, jet-black hair wrapped around metal curlers and pale rose–colored towels hanging on brass hooks. I imagined my nana's heels clicking with each step. Like Dorothy in Emerald City.

In the shade of Sentinel Peak, Nana and Tata's house felt far away from the Presidio, far away from the hustle and bustle of Tucson's tiny downtown. There, in the quiet of her Barrio Menlo home, I asked Nana about her downtown beauty shop, but she

FIGURE 4 Juanita and Tony Peyron in front of El Rapido in the 1940s. Photo from author's personal collection.

always said, *Ay, mijita, I don't remember. When you get old, you can't remember anything.*

My tata Alberto remembered. *Your great-grandfather? Aurelio? He never let her keep the money she earned,* he said, shaking his head as he licked and rolled a thin cigarette at the kitchen table. *Not one nickel, not even the tips!*

My nana didn't say much about her father to me, but instead repeated over and over, *Ay, we worked so hard for him, mijita. We worked so hard.*

Some of Nana's stories weren't stories at all, but more like pictures she painted, with the brittleness of her voice as her brush, little renderings of everything that was made or that she could make, all of creation in her little Barrio Menlo world. Nana pointed to the green iridescence that shone on feathers adorning the hummingbird at her window, or used her hands to show me how the biggest grapefruit hanging from her tree was the circumference of all her fingers stretched wide. Her back patio morning stories brought a calm over me and Ricky. She'd explain how she was planning to cook the fish Tata caught before the sunrise or list all the people she had prayed for the night before, the many hours she'd speak to God on behalf of the sick and poor. She showed us the beads and sequins she painstakingly sewed on to a costume made long ago and recounted the summer when it rained so much that her garden produced flowers she'd never planted, along with a carpet of the most beautiful fuchsia ice plant blossoms she'd ever seen.

Sometimes Nana's memories would get swallowed up and she'd stay silent. She never told us, for example, that in school her teacher renamed her Jenny so that no one had to try to pronounce the name Juanita. Jenny was easier for non-Spanish-speaking teachers and schoolmates to say. Juanita was a name that meant my nana was the complex daughter of a border-crossing tamalero, but Jenny was a girl they better recognized. School friends who later walked into the doors of Juanita's Beauty Shop still called her Jenny and when someone on the street called out that name, she would turn. These are things she never explained to me, but sometimes she whispered things that seemed like they were for my ears only, a story she didn't want anyone but me to hear.

When I was a little girl like you, mijita, I remember my father took me to the fiestas around Easter time. I was having so much fun, you know, just playing and laughing and it was a beautiful fiesta they used to have. Nana painted the air with both hands to illustrate the flowers and decorations she saw. She smiled up into the sky like a bird in bath water. *Ay, que preciosa, las flores, mijita. But I remember one time . . . I saw this man, a big man,* she said. *He was so strong and he was so angry, mijita. He was yelling at his wife something awful. I saw her, a girl with strong legs and hair long to her ankles. Beautiful, beautiful long hair, I remember. And she yelled back at him and everyone at the fiesta watched as that ugly man grabbed her by her hair like this, mira nomás,* she said grabbing my hair by one hand into a pile at the top of my head, *and he dragged her away from the fiesta. She was scream-ing and kicking, that poor girl. Ay, mijita, I had never seen such an ugly thing. I saw him drag her in the dirt by her hair, pobrecita.*

I wondered about what happened to the girl after she was dragged away, but Nana never told that part of the story. I imag-ined Nana was still scared of that man, and I wondered what other stories she had, the ones she wouldn't even whisper.

Long after Juanita's Beauty Shop was closed, Nana still had a beautician's table with gold foil accents and a glass top. She kept it clean and orderly. On Fridays, I couldn't enter the room with the dressing table because it was crowded with all of Nana's sisters, all the tías, waiting to get their color and perm. One by one, they'd rotate positions from the vanity table to the living room chair, to the kitchen, chatting for hours in Spanish that was too fast and too big for me to understand. Ricky and I were shooed away to the garden or to the cuartito where Tata smoked his cigarettes and arranged his tools. But if it wasn't Friday morning, I could sit alone at Nana's vanity and open all the drawers and touch all the things that made her beautiful. I ran her brush through my hair and sprayed aerosol. I pretended until Nana found me in her things. There she combed me and grumbled over my crooked bangs. She made me pretty and told me that someday I'd lose my baby fat. Then, she said, I'd be beautiful like my mother, Anna, used to be, like the day she was a bride—thin and young, with dark, beautiful hair and big eyes smiling under perfectly shaped eyebrows. Nana never failed to mention how thin she was too before she got old. *I only weighed a hundred pounds. Even when I was nine months pregnant, de veras!* she said. She brushed my stringy brown hair with strokes that came both tender and brutal. She combed me stubbornly, like my life depended on it. Like the brush was the way we could both survive. Somehow this was love, warm and sharp with every brush stroke, with every pull and wrangle. I could feel her love on my scalp and on my neck. It was unquestionable.

Bien peinado, Nana led me from the mirror to the kitchen. There she prepared buttered eggs, fideo soup, corn tortillas spread with avocado, and café con Mocha Mix for both me and Ricky. She took us to her garden to watch her birds and to string Texas sage flowers on a needle and thread. All the years that we were in her care, she wore a treasure of cross pendants on her chest and an opal ring on a crooked finger. Ricky and I never saw all her hair turn gray.

Christmas Eve

My father was in his kitchen, his beefy, brown arms in perpetual motion, his pants hanging low beneath a bright-blue apron string, his wrinkled neck holding a gold chain with the Virgen de Guadalupe pendant, she and he both worn and red in the face. His spiral notebook bore the names of each party: Ballesteros, Elías, Carillo, Jacobs, Lopez, Williams, Perez, Brown, Bustamante. Beside each name was the number of dozens ordered by each family. These were tamales for Christmas morning. The numbers added up into the hundreds of dozens a week, all before Christmas Eve. This was the most stressful time of the year for my father. He often yelled at everyone, moved fast, and didn't have a chance to finish his coffee or read the newspaper. On Christmas Eve, my father was a tamal maker. Not a chef, not a businessman, nor a restaurant owner. Not even a cook. He was simply a tamal maker. He prepared the thousands of tamales pulled from their steaming pots, laid them on Styrofoam plates, and wrapped them in clear plastic. He piled each bundle on the counter, and one by one they were carried out the door to be laid out on red-and-green tablecloths in homes all over town, even places out of town and far away from the Presidio.

We came home from the Molino to wash off the masa and chile before the family gathering. We dressed in our Sunday clothes. My mother often had to work on Christmas Eve, but some years she escaped the telephone operator's chair at the Mountain Bell building on East Alameda Street long enough to bring in Christmas with us. Some years she made it home in time to go with us to Uncle Mike's house for the Christmas Eve party. Some years she stayed home and told us to tell the family she was working. By the time we were in high school, Ricky started using this excuse too.

Uncle Mike was the youngest of my nana's siblings, and the only boy of a family with eight older sisters. He was a big man with a big two-story house in a neighborhood pushed up against the saguaro-filled Tucson Mountains on the west side, a quiet cluster of homes between the Santa Cruz River and the Painted Hills Wash. His was the only home almost big enough to fit the whole family, so aunts, uncles, and cousins congregated there each Christmas Eve. In a circle around the living room and under a huge replica of the stone Aztec calendar that hung above the mantel, all my tías sat close to each other. This made it easier to go through the line with our obligatory kisses or hugs. First was Soledad, the oldest, the leader of the family and perhaps the hardest worker. She had a quick wit and a patient heart. Aurelia, who was the kindest, was the only other sister besides my nana Juanita to be married and have a child. My Nana Juanita, the third-born girl, was a creative, a maker. Then there was Maria, who was successful in school and married to a wonderfully tall man named Frank. Maria was one of the first to escape the Molino, becoming a career woman. She didn't have children but had attained a huge collection of porcelain dolls. Angelita, whom we called Angie, was the sister closest to my nana Juanita and often lived with my grandparents during my childhood. She had married Tata Alberto's younger brother Armando (a celebrated war hero and a rancher with a wandering eye), but, tragically, they couldn't have children. Angie persevered through heartache and years of dialysis to treat kidney disease. I remember she ate her tacos with lots of hot salsa and wore oversize wraparound sunglasses all day long. Guadalupe, the sixth born, worked for the Alianza Hispano-Americana, one of the first Mexican American fraternal organizations in the United States, founded in Tucson in 1894. I've been told Guadalupe was engaged at one time, but her father didn't allow her to marry, and so she remained single. She played the piano and never missed attendance at Tucson's annual International Mariachi Conference. Micaela was the smallest, skinniest, and most ostracized of all the sisters. Some people called her slow. She was treated like a child for most of her life, but sometimes she'd sneak a small bill and coins to her nieces in order to secretly purchase her own lipstick and hair curlers. Aurora, whom we called Vory, was the youngest and the handyman of the family. She loved football, talked the loudest, was full of energy, and her sisters questioned her unusual closeness with a woman named Cecilia.

Forming a ring of tongues that switched back and forth between English and Spanish, the eight sisters presented panty hose–covered legs, crossed at the ankles, and freshly permed hair curling around their earlobes. Their gold rings and cross pendants twinkled against dim lights, warming the room. These ladies, my great-aunts, wore bright faces defended in heavy makeup, their chests armored with red-and-green Christmas brooches. They sat in routine arrangements, like the statues in a nativity set that no one but Nana is allowed to touch.

Uncle Mike greeted each guest at the door with a bear hug and a booming voice like a proper car salesman, a career that brought him success when he returned from his service in the army. Unlike his sisters, Uncle Mike was never required to work at the Molino. Maybe it was because he was the boy or maybe it was because he was the baby. Either way, he was spared that labor. He also believed that if he stepped into that kitchen, the molino would probably swallow him, swallow him whole. He kept a safe distance from the family business, and that meant he'd become the first Mexican American to work for a major car dealership in Tucson. He smiled big under bifocals and treated everyone like he had seen us last week instead of last Christmas. In the kitchen, Uncle Mike's wife, my aunt Carmen, quietly checked the slow cooker brimming with whole beans. Carmen was a kind host, and guests in her home were invited to orbit her cloth-covered dining table and then rest in dining chairs pushed up against the wall or on the fireplace benches that looked out over a huge picture window showcasing Tucson's soft city lights.

Nana's buñuelos, perfectly shaped circles of fried cinnamon dough with their thimble cutout centers, sat prominently on the buffet. Ricky and I drenched them in panocha syrup and gobbled them before anyone could catch us. There was a green punch bowl filled with lime sherbet and 7UP. My aunt Yvette or my uncle Tito brought a red velvet cake. When you stared at the table and squinted a bit, the reds and greens would smear and sparkle like a water painting of red chile tamales, ham, beans, rice, and the occasional ambrosia or macaroni salad.

On these nights, my brother, my cousins, and I were all on display like Christmas decorations. We often found ourselves examined by the painted eyes of the tías, and their glances condemned even in silence. Christmas, for this reason, was tinged with anxiety. Would my dress be pretty enough? Was it as pretty as my cousin's? Was it too tight? Had I soiled it with chile dripping from my plate? Did I look fatter than the ham?

Mijita, if it tastes good, you should spit it out, Nana said, though I hoped Christmas would be an exception to her weight-watching advice.

At these family gatherings, my name was mijita. Every one of my aunts and uncles called me this. Every child was named the same: mijito or mijita. With this title, we were easy to identify, to call, to request, to order, and to criticize. With this title, we were endeared no matter what was said of us. No matter if we had stockings that wouldn't stay up, hair that wouldn't stay combed, flies that wouldn't stay zipped, or fingernails that wouldn't stay clean. As mijita, I was unnamed, yet claimed. I was family. About a dozen of us were mijitos and mijitas all at the same time. We belonged to everyone then. We were special, and also not special. We were both.

¡Ay, que cute, mijita! Your dress is so beautiful. Que cute! Be careful not to drip that syrup on it.

Mijita, do a dance for us. But do it good. Dance pretty for your tía Lupe.

¡Ay, mijito! What happened? ¡Ay, no! You better go on a diet!

Ricky hated this. He suffered many of the crueler comments from the tías, even though he was blessed with dimples and light hair. Güerito, my tata called him. For my nana, it seemed that there was no greater gift than a child with blond hair. Even better would have been a slender child with blond hair, but Ricky soon failed on both accounts as he grew into big bones and a dark-brown mane. I'm not sure if Ricky filled his plate back then because he loved tamales so much, or if it was because the pleasure of eating quieted the rattling words from the tías in his head. I know for me it was both. We often went back for seconds. Tamales were piled on a plate like a pyramid. With enough sugary punch, Ricky's mouth chattered a mile a minute and his hair would get messy. Tata would switch to calling him by another nickname: Woodstock. Unfolding tamales one by one, we ate and ate until we were bursting. Soon only empty crumpled ojas filled our plates, evidence of some strange kind of love hammered away into limp leaves stained in red. I don't remember my parents stopping us.

My mother was so well mannered, overly polite with her closed-mouth smiles. At these Christmas parties, she usually stood alone in a floral blouse and dress pants, her hair and eyelashes curled into tendrils around her face. She barely ate and only spoke when spoken to, in her pleasant telephone operator voice. In this way, no one could know what she was thinking. Other years, she wouldn't be there at all. She'd sit in front of the television and eat Christmas dinner alone. My father would talk about the game, then fall asleep on a living room chair, utterly exhausted from Molino work, his arms marked with grease burns, his aching joints finally resting by a fire, those west mountains blanketing us into a moonless desert.

Mr. Rapido

My father, Tony Peyron, tells many stories. All his stories contain some facts and some fiction. Exaggeration is the story, and even though I know this, I believe his stories. I believe him the same way I believe in the things I tell myself.

My grandfather? He was a tough one, man. He was Mr. Rapido. That's what some people called him. And he was a big man. Tall, just like my uncle Mike. Big guy. He would make me and my brother Tito wake up at 5:00 a.m. and start the masa. And if it was the week before Christmas, we would get up at 4:00 a.m. Then we wouldn't finish until late at night. He was a good guy, though. He was good to his customers, ya know what I mean? In the summer, he would take us in his 1933 Dodge Plymouth to Nogales to buy the elotes. He'd fill it up so that you couldn't see out the back! Barely had room to get in the car with all the corn. Man! We were itching with the corn silk all the way home! And you know, hey, let me tell you something . . . he'd drive like a mad man. He got that name Mr. Rapido because he was the fastest cab driver in Mexico City.

My father's voice gets louder as the story goes along. He checks to make sure you're listening to him by saying your name between sections of each story. Or sometimes he says, *Hey!*, and hits you on the back while he's talking or grabs your wrist to hold your attention.

One time I accepted money from a customer, you know? Boy, did my grandfather scold me good. Hey, no one was allowed to hold the money but him, you know what I mean?

There is a back-and-forth. The good and the ugly get mixed up in his memories. What he really tells is a story about the way we talk about the dead. His story, his spoken words have something to prove. That we loved. That we hurt. It all gets mixed in together like a batter bowl that swirls by itself on the countertop.

There was this ranch on the way back to Tucson and a lady who lived there who made the best food, ah man. It didn't matter what time we left; he would make sure he got us to that ranch by lunchtime. My father points to his invisible watch. *We'd come back downtown, and he'd make me carry a big sack of elotes all over the neighborhood. "¿Eres hombre o no eres hombre?" he'd ask me. A million times he asked me that. Hey, he worked us hard. There were no breaks. When I'd get that big sack to someone's front door, he'd be the one to ring the bell and ask the people if they needed any corn. They always said hi to him and offered him food. They loved him. The people loved my grandfather. Everyone. But it was because he was good to them, you know what I mean? Any time of day, if they needed something from the store, he would go take it to them. Masa, tortillas, anything. He sold the masa for ten cents a pound. TEN CENTS a pound! Can you believe that? And everyone said that his was the best masa in town. Because he was the only person in the neighborhood with a molino, and he shared it with everybody. Everybody had credit, man! He had a deal with every guy in town. He was a tender guy, ya know? He'd give me and* Tito *a quarter for half a day's work and then we were the richest kids in town, boy! We'd get that quarter and go to the Fox Theatre for a double feature and the biggest sucker they had.* My father pretends he has a lollipop, licks the air. Then he stares down at the ground, at nothing. He holds the picture in his mind as long as he can. In this way, Aurelio is made alive over and over for my father, like a replay. Aurelio is in the flesh. In bright lights like a movie star. In charge of the room. The bags of masa are heavy. The seats of the Fox Theatre are plush red velvet. My father's memory grows slow like a saguaro. Stories take decades, with lots of space and time in between.

He made us work. He expected work out of everyone. He had these catering jobs with the City of Tucson and the electric company. Every year, man. He'd do all their parties and me and Tito *would serve with him. I was just about five years old when I started catering. I walked out there into those big ballrooms with that tray of Mexican hot chocolate and pan de huevo. Then I'd sneak back in the kitchen and take a bite out of that sweet bread. Man, it was best. Everything tasted better back then, you know?*

The bread is plush like the seats at the Fox Theatre. It is dusted with granules of sugar. It is shaped like half-moons and full moons with tiny mountains and valleys. Bread like this is a whole meal. Dense. Anise spiced. Softened with steamed milk and chocolate. This is bread to eat together. Aurelio can eat a half dozen, according to Tony Peyron. Bread called conchas, elotes, orejas, ojos de buey. Can anyone eat that much? Can anyone be so hungry as to devour the whole moon? Shells like giant clams, whole ears of corn, the entire piglet, an ear, can anyone swallow a bull's-eye? Wash it down with cream and cocoa?

And the next day, he'd have us at it again. We'd sit down with that gunnysack of beef and start cutting. Man, he loved meat. You know, he had a huge tattoo of a cross on his arm? Huge. And that's the arm he used when he'd wring a chicken's neck. He'd swing it around in circles, pobrecito, the little chicken. And there you go. Dinner. He'd sit down in a little dining room chair and start plucking the feathers. Man, I don't know how he even fit in those chairs. He was so big. Then after working on the chicken, he'd get up and start dancing like a boxer. Around and around. Aw man, he loved to dance. And he'd play like I was in the ring with him.

My father's stories step in one decade and turn around in another. His words move fast. It is hard to keep pace with him. I get twisted in his recollections. I confuse right and left, but I've come to realize his memory is a clock moving fast-forward. Rewind. And fast-forward again.

Yeah, he loved that Dodge Plymouth. He'd take us to the cornfields and we'd fill it up with elotes. He'd drive through and throw the ears of corn in the back with me and Tito. And he'd drive so fast! He'd go through there and shout, "¡PILÓN!" We were itching all over, you know what I mean? And I remember the time he took us down there shopping in México. He bought a big ol' copper pot to cook his chicharrones. My father holds his arms out like he's hugging the pot. *Man, you shoulda seen it! We came home on the Greyhound bus that time and the copper pot took up half the bus. Hey!* He grabs my elbow. *I'm not kidding! Those chicharrones were so good.* My father hits his fist on the table. *Real pork, you know. Real hogs raised on a real farm. I remember him dipping the skins and bringing them out so crispy. And salty. Man!*

My father's memories never reveal that Aurelio was from a tiny town called Atemajac de Brizuela. When I search for it, I find a town in the state of Jalisco, a place near water with buildings that look like an antique Tucson. It is a place with markets on every corner. But my father doesn't seem to know it. Instead, Tony Peyron spins the same tales over and over and most of them happen in a much bigger city, Mexico City, where (for my father) Aurelio is a taxi driver. In his last interpretation, Aurelio has a brother my father has never mentioned before. He drives a taxi too. I imagine brothers circling the city in yellow, their cabs filled with faces and elotes that multiply until the whole town is a maze of siblings. I don't know how many Mr. Rapidos are out there in the world, winding around old dirt roads in yellow cabs. I don't know what parts of my father's stories are true and what parts came from his imagination. I just know that they taste real. The meat is real, from real animals on a real ranch. The flavors are not a lie. The fields of corn and beans and pumpkins are no dream. I can smell them. And I can't smell them when anyone else has ever tried to tell me about Aurelio. About how he wore atomic-yellow neckties. How he jumped up in his bed every time the cat ran across the piano keys in the middle of the night. How he once put out a fire in the zaguan by urinating on it. These other stories might be closer to fact than my father's, but my father's fiction is what usually rolls off my own tongue. Somehow, over meals and over kitchen counters, the stories have moved from his mouth to mine.

Perez Birth

like twins came
a brother breach
a red thread capsicum
around the wrist

a name like volcano work
a place where the mourning scrape
one of you will be first
one of you will withdraw
your mother was at the end of her rope
but I am
her braid in the canyon

—el pensamiento

The Stork's Nest

Nana Juanita points to her toes to explain why some are piled on top of each other, twisted and overlapping, because tortillas don't earn enough for new shoes on growing girl's feet. Her toes remind me of Tito's legs, warped and wet, wrangled out from Nana's womb at the Stork's Nest.

FIGURE 5 Juanita, Tito, and Tony Peyron in front of their apartment in Barrio Presidio in 1945. Photo from author's personal collection.

Nana tells me about her mother, Martina, about how she worked at the Stork's Nest helping women deliver their babies while also working at the Molino and while working at her own stove to feed all her own babies—nine born between El Paso and Tucson among the fields or copper mines. Nana says her mother *died of lung cancer, mijita. Such a hard life, ay, pobrecita.* Nana says, *¿Mi mamá? She made tortillas every day, mijita.* Every day, *de veras,* tortillas so round you could use them for geometry homework. Nana says Martina *had such a hard life, you know, she was a harsh woman, mijita,* from Zacatecas, and *¡Ay, her calditos, mijita!* Nana says, *sus calditos, they were the best because they were made with nothing, can you imagine?* Soup so empty, almost clear. Warm, rich nothing. Poor, *poor caldito.*

The Stork's Nest was around the corner from the Molino, so Martina's commute was a one-minute walk. She did eight-hour shifts for Mrs. Jacobs, the proprietor, who had lost her own daughter in childbirth. I imagine Martina was there when Nana labored on one of the ten or more beds at the Stork's Nest. Both Tito and Tony were churned out, pushed and pushed like a sunrise, like freshly bathed corn, at the Stork's Nest. Tito's legs came out *crippled, pobrecito,* Nana said, *and I had to give him exercises each day. But your daddy. Tony was lucky, gracias a Dios. Born lucky, güerito, güerito, with blond hair, can you imagine?* Sprouting straight legs that ran in straight lines down the football field. Nana was his cheerleader in the bleachers, shouting out loud like labor pains for her Tony, for cream skin, for brown eyes. Tony running in circles, always with food in his mouth, lucky, Martina's calditos and tortillas turning and churning over in his lucky little mouth.

Nana points to an imaginary corner of the zaguan in the old house. After tortillas and after calditos, after babies came out clean, Nana says Martina sat in her chair in her corner of the zaguan smoking cigarettes, one after the other. *She held her arms crossed over her chest, like this, mijita,* like eternal rest. She rolled her own, of course, and I can see that little rolled cigarette hanging between long, wrinkled digits, fingernails long and sharp like Nana's. I can see a crooked trail of smoke rising like a mist of steam from the hoya, translucent and warm, nothing.

A Few White Lies

I want to believe all the stories, but my mother's words ring in my head: *Everything that comes out of your father's mouth . . . I can't tell if it is the truth or a lie.*

I tuck my doubt quickly under a roll of flesh so no one can see. I'm sure even when I die, I won't be naked, so no one in my family will find my disbelief hidden along with the licked-clean bowls of food I wasn't supposed to eat.

Anyway, all the people who can confirm these stories are dead and gone. I won't find what is true before my bones dry up, so there will be tiny morsels of faith, if anything, in stories and sometimes there will be no faith at all. A faith famine will fill up my closets and dressers and bedroom corners. There will be a bounty of questions. And sometimes, when I want it to be true badly enough, I will blindly believe every contradictory thing my family says to me.

Brother Stories

My father says my great-grandfather Aurelio had a twin brother named Francisco. For my father, he is like a second Mr. Rapido.

The brothers arrived in Tucson together. They saved up their money to buy the house at 220 North Meyer and open the store in the Presidio together. Francisco, the elder, was going to travel by train to Los Angeles with all the money they had left—all their savings from peddling tortillas and tamales, barrio a barrio from D.F. to El Paso to Bisbee to Tucson. Francisco would buy the equipment needed for the new business. He would find the molino stones. He would come home with volcanic rock for grinding. He left at dawn, but Aurelio found out that Francisco never got on the train, and instead his truck was gone.

Francisco never came back. No one here knows why. No one can answer my one thousand questions about brothers. Did they long to see him? Did they long to save him?

My father and his father do not search after brothers. They search for gold. They trade metal detector tricks. They dream about finding. They dream of jackpots. In much older stories, there are promises of gold in the mountains. It is there waiting; all we have to do is go and get it, they say. I want to believe these stories about hidden treasures and lost brothers, testaments to an inheritance born in 1933. I imagine an alternate Mr. Rapido universe where there is no water and where there are no stones turning and turning. I imagine a hollow place where the grinding has stopped.

Sleepy Subjects

In 1928, when my great-grandparents Aurelio and Martina were stopped in Bisbee on their way to settling in Tucson, Diego Rivera, the famed Mexican muralist, met his soon-to-be wife, the artist Frida Kahlo. That same year, Rivera painted *El sueño (La noche de los pobres) / Sleep (The Night of the Poor)*. The image depicts a group of men, women, and children in a tight frame, sleeping on the floor against a wall, nestled together under an archway. These subjects are so tired, so fatigued, that their sleep can't wait, not for bedrooms or beds or comfortable conditions. Sleep is, itself, the comfort.

When I see Rivera's sleepers, these dreamers, I think of Aurelio and Martina. I imagine them with all their daughters in tow, moving from border town to border town, finally arriving in the Old Pueblo. I imagine them asleep together on their way, in tiny bedrooms, in hallways, in the desert, along rivers, on long bus rides and in packed truck beds. I imagine them on their way to a dream of a big adobe house in the center of town. A dream of the molino grinding away and tamales and tortillas and enough of everything. For everyone.

Before their deaths, Diego Rivera and Frida Kahlo didn't create images of rest.

A few days before she died in 1954, Frida Kahlo finished her last work, *Viva la Vida, Watermelons*. Three years later, Rivera painted *The Watermelons* as his last work, just before his own death. Both pieces depict whole and large segments of the fruit on a table, sliced, bitten, or carved, revealing green-marbled fruit skins, bright-white strips of rind, blush and crimson flesh dotted with black seeds.

Rivera died a few months before my great-grandmother Martina died of cancer on February 11, 1958. My great-grandfather Aurelio would die, unexpectedly, fifteen months later.

FIGURE 6 Aurelio and Martina Perez in front of their Barrio Menlo home in the mid–1950s. Photo from author's personal collection.

Barrio Call

Just imagine, mijita. May 11, 1959, Menlo Park Neighborhood, Tucson.

———————

Hair is wrapped taut over Velcro curlers, covered by headscarves whipping lime-green and flamingo-pink swirls behind ears. Hands squeeze half-soaked tissues tight in the pockets of housedresses. The neighbors leave green garden hoses running over front-yard flower beds. The temperature will reach ninety-three degrees. The phone is ringing, calling news of a last supper. It is not good news, and it stretches out over the barrio mountains pulled across the horizon.

———————

Aurelio Perez died, informs a neighbor over the phone, without as much as a buenos días.
 Yeah, I heard already.
 Oh, you already heard, huh?
 Si pues, la Vory . . . su hija, she came over to tell la comadre de mi otra vecina.
 Ah, OK.
 Poor guy.
 Pobrecito.
 You know how old he was? Seventy, creo.
 Que lástima.
 I know, pues, he looked real good, you know, when I saw him last. Over there walking to Juanita's, I saw him. He looked real good.

And did they tell you how it happened?

Well, Vory said something. Dice que . . . no se . . . it was in his sleep or when he was laying down or something like that.

¿De veras?

———————

Si, pero . . .

What?

They said it was because of something he ate.

¡Ay, no!

They say it was the watermelon.

What watermelon?

Well, he ate a whole watermelon right before, dicen.

What do you mean a whole watermelon?

The whole thing. And a big supper too. Can you imagine?

Ay, no. Then he died?

Si. Luego murió.

¡No me digas!

De verdad.

Ay, que lástima.

I know.

———————

Maybe it was poisoned. Or rotten. You think?

No, it had to be fresh fruit. Juanita wouldn't give it to him rotten.

Well, and he ate the whole thing, ¿que no?

Y entonces, pues . . . the death certificate. I dunno what went wrong.

What about the death certificate?

El médico no sabe nada.

What are you talking about? Did he write about the poison?

That's the thing. He wrote in the box "natural causes."

Oh really?

But he crossed that out, el médico—

Ay, no . . . it WAS poison . . . ay, pobrecito! The watermelon killed him!

Nooo. He crossed it out, then he wrote something else.

What?! What did he write?

He crossed it out and wrote "error."

¿Cómo?

He wrote the word "error" and then he wrote something else in the box, but no one can read it.

What do you mean no one can read it?

Nobody can read it, te digo. It's just a wavy line. No one knows what it says.

¡Pinche médicos que no pueden escribir por nada! Well, call him up, pues! Ask him!

We tried.

¿Y?

They hung up on us.

Who hung up?

The lady that works at the office. Y ella no sabe nada.

I'm gonna walk over to that guy's office right now. We need some answers! What if it was poison? What if Menlo is being poisoned?

Ay, no. You better not. I mean, think of the family. They've got enough with all the funeral plans. You know, las flores, el traje, y todo. Let them mourn. Let them be at peace. Don't make a big fuss. Déjelos. Leave them in peace.

Ahh. Maybe you're right.

Nobody eats a whole watermelon.

I guess maybe it was bad. There was something bad in it, don't you think?

It was poison, pues.

Sí, creo.

Pobrecito. I better go buy some candles, ahorita.

OK, well. I gotta call the neighbors on the other side too so they know why there are so many cars. The driveway might be blocked again. Y con el calor hoy, hijuela. I don't wanna stand out there all day telling people to move their cars when they are in mourning.

OK, pues.

Ándale, pues.

Ándale.

¿Pero sabes que? I didn't ever know that you could die from that.

From what?

La sandía entera.

true vine

it was the Seed that saved
after that fruit was eaten

it was a woman who harvested
my promise

she delivered to this world
the Hope sweeter
than red than gold
fruit flesh swollen with water from the garden hose

so
when grandfathers and great-grandfathers perish
when seeds are scattered like tears and slander
think on me your thoughts of fathers
your green victory your summer bounty
your watermelons fat with pleasure

—*el pensamiento*

I'll tell you what they say happened

They say it came after Francisco Vázquez de Coronado prayed to San Juan Bautista, the patron saint of water. The river was drying up, and they were desperate. That's when they say the rain came. Coronado was on the banks of the Santa Cruz River, June 24, 1540, which happened to be San Juan's feast day. They say the end was near when, finally, San Juan had mercy on them. Water flowed.

Ever since, June 24 marks the beginning of our monsoon season. It has to, they say, because prayers were answered. But I've been in the habit of questioning prayers answered, so I don't know what to think about Coronado and his legend and all these things they say.

I'll admit—I'm no different. I've wanted miracles. I've even prayed for water.

As a child, I prayed to see snow falling outside my bedroom window. I wanted snow on the saguaros and snow on the nopales. To be sure, I supplemented prayers with wishes at coin fountains, in front of birthday candles, and while witnessing falling stars. I guess I wanted to cover my bases. Which is probably a sign that I never believed my prayers would work in the first place. I know I've been just like Coronado wandering lost in this desert looking for a treasure that probably doesn't exist. I've thought, *Maybe.* Then again. Maybe he and I have prayed the wrong way to the wrong god. Maybe our words only bring us to the same dry riverbank, year after year.

Many people like to call these circles *a journey*. They say our repeating words are simply an expedition. But these repetitions mean that I end up in the same place as where I began—a scorched-earth pueblo. And when all the repeated words go up like smoke, I still feel hungry. Thirsty. Like Coronado's men, I go on a rampage. When there is nothing at the bottom of the well, I plunder. In search of gold and silver treasures, I find myself where I don't belong; I find myself clawing at corn and beans.

I'll tell you what didn't happen

I did not make it to the water. The Santa Cruz was dry by the time I was born. The water may never come back, but everyone still calls it a river.

Other things didn't happen. The water was there when my father and my uncle Tito were boys, but Tito never got to swim in its pools. He was in leg braces, and it would have been difficult to manage the mile walk from Barrio Menlo to the river. He was far from healing water. His miracle never happened that way.

I know Nana prayed repeatedly. I think she talked to God even more than she talked to me. Every night she prayed at an altar she made on top of her white French colonial bedroom dresser, the one she called her cajón. There were photographs on her altar, and synthetic flowers. Candles were lit and tiny statues of saints stared back at me from the dresser top, their faces filled with longing. Near her bedroom window facing the black mountain, her words circled like a dust storm.

There were other interventions. There were moments when Nana and Tata trusted Tito's legs to a doctor or a procedure or an herb-infused bath. My father remembers surgeries were performed.

Oh yeah, he tells me, *I remember waving to* Tito *at his window. He was way up there on the third floor of St. Mary's Hospital!*

Because my father can't be trusted, I have to ask: Does the hospital have three floors?

And anyhow, there were no miraculous healings. Tito never stood up from a hospital bed to run out of St. Mary's, tackling and punting like my father.

All these things that didn't happen might be a fair reason for me to think no one was listening to Nana's prayers any more than one was listening to my petitions for snow.

In moments of confusion, I wonder if our stories of miraculous rain and lame men walking are no more real than tales of talking rabbits, deer, and hummingbirds. Lame men don't walk, I protest. I act like I'm my own god most of the time. And I make up my own stories, though they end up being the kind that only try to erase the stories that already exist. I call this one "Dia de San Juan":

———————

Tito sets aside a pencil drawing of a cactus wren on his bedside table. The dotted bird's wings need a bolder edge, he thinks, but there is no time. He hears the boys leaving. He has been waiting for this day, imagining himself wading and floating in the river with them. Like them. He knows it is dangerous, but it could be worth it. And the men and women have all feasted on watermelon and fresh cuts of beef from the fire and are too sleepy and distracted to prevent his escape.

A small gang of boys carve a path through the quelites. He tries to keep up but follows their quick and chaotic parade from a distance that ensures no one will punish him with menacing taunts and kicks to the shin. They've hurt him before in more ways than one.

He loses his balance once or twice. No matter. He can feel the rocks through the soles of his shoes and they assure him. His glasses slip off, but he doesn't stop.

When he reaches the Santa Cruz, he hides himself on its banks in exhaustion and watches his little brother and the other Menlo boys splashing in the water. Their legs are slick with mud. He is a boy bound to his home most days, comforted by comic books and quiet imagining. He has practiced these comforts on the city bus and in the hospital bed. He has stared out of windows more than most boys his age.

But today is special. Tito has reason to believe this day is holy enough to bring change. Then, just as the water gushes and bubbles hard in the Santa Cruz, Tito sees a figure appear in the tall grass beside the cottonwood. Tito is not startled, half expecting this vision. *Do you want to be well?* the figure asks.

I'll tell you what did happen

By junior high school, some of the boys from Menlo befriended Tito, and they fought for him each time a bully came near. My father remembers the day his leg braces came off too. He couldn't walk straight or upright, but he moved on his own, a paraplegic not bound to a wheelchair.

In his junior and senior years, Tito won Tucson High School's Eastman Kodak photo contest multiple times. Most of his subjects were of the natural world, images of sunsets, mountains, and rivers. In the frame there were often silent rabbits, deer, and hummingbirds. When I stare out of the window for long periods of time now, I can see why photography would come easily to him.

Tito opened a photography shop on Congress Street after high school. He slept there most nights, though the Old Pueblo ghosts kept him from rest. One day, a woman from Texas came into his shop. She wore her blond hair in a big beehive and chatted for an hour with Tito. She asked him where the best nightclubs were, and he offered to take her. They danced, and that's when he fell in love with her.

More importantly, Tito danced.

They had a short marriage. Estranged from him, she was ill and died a young death back in Texas a few years after they met. He never got to see her again.

Tito eventually closed the photo shop, but he kept snapping images. Everyone in my family has Tito's work displayed in their home. His pictures are different now than they were in high school. There are no more right angles or straight edges. Instead, he develops his images on cuts of flagstone, a craft matched by no other photographer we've ever heard of. Portraits are his specialty. He creates rock slabs with an image burned into the sand grain, faces developed on the smooth surface of cemented quartz. His work doesn't include perfect squares or rectangles like the ones in those comic book stories he used to read. Each of his flat-rock photos has a jagged edge that reminds me of a broken window frame.

I'll tell you what I tell myself

San Juan Bautista was in a river when a familiar figure appeared at its banks, and he saw miracles there by the water. But when he later found himself in a dark prison cell, Juan wondered if it had all been real. Was it his imagination? He asked for the truth and an answer was delivered to him within those prison walls. The answer that came by messenger was simply this: *The lame walk.*

I am still waiting for what must be the truth. In the meantime, I tell myself I can keep imagining healings and miracles. I can paint them like murals on a wall or capture them like images in Polaroid frames. I can see Tito dancing, his feet floating above the ground, weightless.

FIGURE 7 Six of the Perez sisters—Soledad, Aurelia, and Guadalupe (*top row, left to right*), and Angelita, Juanita, and Maria (*bottom row, left to right*)—with Tito in front of Juanita's Beauty Shop in the early 1940s. Photo from author's personal collection.

santa cruz

someday you will go to water
taste and see
you are made
this will be
the beginning of your wanting
to be well

you will sunset sit
beneath mesquite limbs
blowing
birthday candle hope tossing
coins in fountains for
a dream prayer answer

a feast without beheadings
a platter
perfect round manna
snow sifted down
from our father in heaven

who hears you
who knows your heart and the hearts
of all who come down to the river

—*el pensamiento*

PART III

Reflection

There were two painted plaster antiques from the early twentieth century that hung on the wall in the old house. Two brown faces with headdresses shining green and red and gold. They had only heads and no bodies, but all day and all night they faced each other, like mirror reflections.

Though I admired them, I also feared their gaze. As a child, I didn't realize they were caricatures for a marketing scheme, advertisements for shops that sold cigars or tobacco products. But my family didn't use them that way. They were never in the storefront space and never in full view of customers. They were placed in the center of the old house, in the zaguan, where only family and friends could view them. And they watched over us all, in our comings and goings. They didn't close their eyes nor turn away from each other or from us.

One day, my father came home from work at the Molino and told us one of the plaster wall hangings had fallen and shattered. He didn't know how it happened. He opened the front door of the old Molino house early one morning and found all the broken pieces scattered over the floor. It was as if some strange wind had crept in under the floorboards to knock that head off the wall. Some pieces sprayed under locked doors and would not be redeemed. My father was sad about it, shaking his head. They didn't belong to him, but in his eyes, this was a tragic loss. They must be very valuable, he thought. I wondered if he was responsible for that value. Or entitled to it. Or connected to it. Perhaps the heads meant something to him that he hadn't talked to me about, something no one in my family talked about.

When I first walked into the old house after this blow, I understood why my father was so shocked. It was unsettling to see one profile left hanging on the wall, facing only a faded outline of its other half. In all the years I walked the zaguan, in and out of the old house, back and forth to the Molino, never once had I considered that those faces might not hang there looking at each other, forever.

germination

some seeds
fall among the thorns
and those thorns swallow up
the spring
winding words
tangling little children who have heard
choking them out
of bloom

—el pensamiento

Beneath Blankets

Sometimes Ricky and I try to take back the sleep we lost when woken too early out of our beds and into the morning grind. We sleep in places where everyone is working and where no one else is allowed to sleep. Whether skies are dark or bright, we are covered in blankets—thick, plaid, wool, Mexican.

Sleep happens in front of the El Rapido mural, along the ruins of the Presidio wall. Parked on Washington Street on school mornings, before sunrise, the cab of my father's truck is as quiet as a predawn bedroom. Truck sleeping is preceded by bed sleeping as Ricky and I lie side by side on a full-size bed under Nana's crocheted covers. When it is still pitch dark, my father enters my room and turns on my bedside lamp. He picks me up and holds me, rocking me awake. I don't remember if he ever does this to Ricky. I awake to the smell of the lamp's bulb burning dust and moth. On some cold nights, the three of us sleep together on the living room floor by the fireplace. I am excited to camp there. Ricky remembers this also. It is not so much a story we tell each other but a memory we share. A memory of sleep.

Even in summer, when the evening monsoons darken the skies before the sunset, we pretend the storms make it cold enough to need thick Mexican blankets, purchased in Tijuana or Nogales, hauled from the border to our home on a hill. Ricky and I wrap ourselves in their plaid patterns and watch the lightning storms from our porch. We pretend to sleep, or pretend to be sleepy, but our eyes stay wide, waiting for each bolt that seems to rock the whole house, the sound cracking the sky in half.

In the morning, we carry blankets. They come with us to the cab of my father's truck. Sometimes we share one blanket between us. Sometimes I sleep, and sometimes I close my eyes under the blanket on Washington. My father opens the kitchen and pours raw pinto beans into pots of water. Ricky and I slumber in the quiet cab of a truck while my father's hands labor at the molino.

Ricky and I sleep while the mixer turns and pots simmer. My father works us some mornings, but often he lets us alone to huddle beneath blankets. In the hotter months, we leave the truck and rest on any flat surface in the kitchen, atop freezers or stainless steel tables. We sleepwalk between the blue flame of gas burners and the water streaming from long arched faucets. We dream, then we wake to the grinding sound of the molino.

$1

Here, taste it, my father says as he holds a forkful up to my face. *Hey, I'm telling you. I'm not kidding—this is the best one I've ever tasted. You gotta try it!*

No, I don't want it.

What's wrong with you? he says, shocked at my rejection. *Try it, will you!*

I don't want to.

Eat it now! he shouts, half playing and half not playing.

Why? Why do I have to?

Just do as I say. Hurry up. Eat it! But I refuse and move to the other side of the table. His jaw drops for a moment, then he turns back to his plate and takes another bite. *This is the best I've ever had. I mean it,* he says, chewing hard now, making the food pay for my rebuff. He swallows, then changes tactics. *Please?* he says softly, *I'll give you a dollar if you take just one bite.*

I shake my head and keep my lips closed tightly.

Come on! You don't know what you're missing! Come. Here. Now.

Popovers

My father is our priest in a pickup truck. He smells like corn and grease and Coors Light. He pastors over us, teaching us his own way of knowing. And by this catechism there is, like the wind, an almost invisible beginning.

It is Sunday morning and my mother is home from work. She is sleeping after a night shift at the phone operator's switchboard. She must not be disturbed, so my father puts Ricky and me in the truck and drives us out to the reservation a few miles south of our home. On the drive, we see the bright-white San Xavier del Bac Mission punch through the woodland of mesquite trees and push against gray mountains and blue sky. We park in the dirt lot and drag our feet over gravel walkways up to the church founded by the Jesuit missionary Padre Eusebio Francisco Kino. Made of piled stone and mud, the mission's bell towers rise up like siblings, one done and one undone. The taller tower is domed, marking its place in the desert like an inverted exclamation point.

My father points at the mission's façade and retells his same ancient tale. *You see the cat and mouse?* he says, not really asking.

I can't see it, I say.

Where? Ricky asks.

Open your eyeballs! my father badgers. He points a crooked finger at the elaborate carved mud plaster. His heavy hand lands on the crown of our heads to force our gaze up higher. Eventually, we find the sculptural details: a skinny cat, an elusive mouse emerging from the baroque background.

When the cat catches the mouse, the world will end, he says, resigned like a prophet.

How's it gonna catch the mouse? Ricky asks, loud and suspicious. There is never a clear answer. All that seems to matter to my father is the story, the words repeated like an incantation. When we step inside the vestibule, my father dips fingers into a bowl of holy water and makes the sign of the cross on his forehead, heart, and shoulders, and Ricky and I repeat after him.

This is baptism.

My head tilts back as we walk in farther and I stumble on uneven floors. We walk deeper into the mission, making even our footsteps as quiet as we can. In the mortuary chapel, Ricky and I kneel and repeat our memorized lines. My father gives us coins to place in the collection box so we can light a candle to add to the glow of the sanctuary. I light my candle, and Ricky lights his. Then we watch the flames glow among all the rest, making light in the darkness of the shrine. Only then are we cleansed from the sin of skipping Sunday Mass.

This is reconciliation.

I look to the statue of the Virgen, her palms facing up into the blue hue of the nicho engulfing her. I say something, a Hail Mary. I try not to think about whether or not she hears me. I wonder instead if she is asleep, eyes open. I think if I were her, I'd get tired listening to all these repetitions. Still, I like coming to the mission. I like going through these clunky and absent-minded steps, mostly because I already know they will be sealed with a meal at the fry bread stands.

Other people call them fry bread, but my father calls them popovers. In front of the mission, the people who make them call themselves the Tohono O'odham. He is often demanding of servers in restaurants, but he acts differently with the ladies who stand all morning long wrapped in aprons, their hands waving over cauldrons of oil, their palms turning dough over and over. They say Padre Kino was the one to bring the wheat—both a blessing and a curse—here to the desert people. My father couldn't be happier. We walk away from the cat and mouse and come to the edge of the parking lot, where the expectation of fry bread is the only thing keeping my father from chattering too much. In line for popovers, he is eager but more restrained, quieter. What he waits for is quite valuable. The dough bubbling and glistening gold is sanctified. When it finally arrives warm in his hands, he takes a bite, then passes the plate to me, and I eat. I pass it to Ricky, and he eats. Holding the bread to our lips, we are anointed by honey slinking down our fingers, down to our elbows.

This is communion.

My father shakes his head back and forth in praise of popovers. Mouth full, he mumbles something I don't quite hear, but I know exactly what he means. I know changing Kino's wheat into fry bread is some kind of alchemy. Like making water into wine. Desert people know how to make one thing into something else. It happens every day. Popovers consecrated in honey or powdered sugar or chile colorado nest in paper plates in front of the mission. This becomes holy ground, where the city meets reservation, and there is transfiguration dotted with the round and bubbled faces of fry bread.

This is worship.

I learn slowly. In my memory, my father drives us out to the mission over and over. We repeat this ritual many times, until eventually the thought of popovers becomes a direct message to me, a story. In the story, there is a sacrifice—but it isn't mine. In the story, there is blood. There are thorns and tears painted on the walls and carved into rocks. But it is a story I forget too. Under the saguaro rib ramada at the mission, I begin to feel unstable on those gravel rocks. Just when I think I know what I am and where I come from, the ground shifts again. I stare at my half-eaten popover and squeeze it tight so the wind doesn't take it away.

Choking

Your daddy almost died, mijita, my tata says as he cuts thin slices of steak on a plate for Ricky and I to share. *So you have to chew it good, OK, mijito? Chew it real good.*

He slices meat with a small knife that has come back from fishing and hunting trips with microscopic specks of deer or catfish blood.

It's true, mijita, he insists.

The three of us sit in the smoke-filled room watching our plates steam, and Tata begins the story again.

My father almost died in my nana's kitchen—a place where nothing dies. It is the kitchen where I spoke my first word: apple, because a decorative ceramic plate hanging on the wall presented three pieces of painted fruit. Nana's kitchen is where I took my first steps, up on my toes like a dancer. And it is the setting for Tata's story about the time Tony almost missed the chance to become my father, and so it is my story too. I am part of my father's skin and blood and lips and tongue in this story, though they are the parts of me not yet born. And because it is my story too, I want to listen to Tata say it over and over. I want to chew, chew, chew.

He was sitting right there where you are sitting, mijo, he says, gesturing to the wooden chair where Ricky's feet dangle. *And we were eating carne asada too,* he says. Tata's mustache is the color of salt and pepper and it curls over the corners of his mouth. He holds a tortilla in his right hand and his chile güerito in the left. On the rare occasion when he has to go out to eat, he takes that fat yellow pepper wrapped in a small paper towel or stretch of plastic wrap tucked into his shirt pocket. If he forgets his chile, he has to turn the car around and go back for it.

Was Tito there? I wonder out loud.

Of course your uncle Tito was there. He was sitting right there where you are sitting, mijita. He saw the whole thing.

I imagine Tito in my chair, his legs bound in metal braces, dangling like rusty machine parts tossed in a pile.

Tata shakes his head and takes another bite. *It was awful,* he says, still chewing. *Tony was always too hungry. You know, your father was always shoveling the food in and never chewing it like he should. He was always in a big hurry.*

I wonder if this is because Nana's cooking is so good, or because his hunger makes him worry someone might come along to take his food away. Maybe my father was born in a hurry, I think. His running around reminds me of the hyperactive boys in my kindergarten class who kick me as we wait in line for the pencil sharpener, boys who want to exchange boredom for a dangerous game.

Juice from a bite falls onto Tata's flannel shirt and with the bouquet of tobacco and coffee grounds already there, it is absorbed deep into the fibers. Tata stands up, stiff and halfway bent over, arms behind him. He limps toward the gas stove to warm another tortilla.

We were eating our carne asada, real happy, he says, *and we saw Tony get up from his chair and run around the kitchen in circles.* Tata flips his tortilla twice over the fire, good and toasted. *We thought he was playing, you know? He was never sitting still, Tony. We didn't know what was happening. Nana was yelling at him to sit down and eat with us.* This sounded perfectly reasonable to us. We were accustomed to seeing my father running around in circles in his own kitchen.

And then I saw Tony's face. And it was blue, Tata says, shaking his head and sitting down again to his plate with his warm tortilla.

I imagine a face filled in with blue crayon, dark-blue cheeks, and light-blue lips. I think about a purple-blue forehead and turquoise eyes. Ricky and I ask excited questions as though this is our first time hearing the story and the smoke from Tata's burned tortilla edges dissolves into the sacred air above Nana's gas stove.

He puts his tortilla and his chile güerito down for the big ending.

What did I do? he says, standing up again. *I grabbed Tony real tight and I opened up his mouth real big like a fish. Like this,* he says as he shows us his fist reaching into the air, *and I put my hand down his throat and I pulled out that big chunk of meat.*

We watch Tata's mustache smile, and we settle further into the mud walls and linoleum floor of Nana's kitchen, like none of us will ever leave this room. Tata's warning stomps down on me like hooves from a ranch horse buried long ago. I know well enough. We are like Tony. We are not exempt from taking too big a bite.

Buñuelos

Nana clears the table just days before Christmas, and the oil is heated to the correct temperature. In a room no bigger than ten feet by ten feet, she fits a refrigerator; a stove with range and hood; a microwave; cabinets holding dishes for an army; a trash can; a round oak dining table with four chairs; a ceiling-high hutch holding all kinds of important papers, cookies, and tools; a door to the garden; a window over the sink; decorative plates hanging on the walls; herself; my tata; and as many as four can't-sit-still grandchildren all at once.

She wipes down the table with soapy water, then a dry paper towel patterned with pink flowers. She swipes a handful of flour across the table, and it immediately forms into a winter playground, complete with mountain ranges, ski slopes, and snow angels of my dreams. My finger draws *MELAN* into the flour before I run out of room at the table edge.

Nana makes tiny doughballs, dotted with anise, and lines them up on the winter playground. Each of equal proportion, they move quickly from her warm hands to the snow. Tempted beyond what we believe to be our capacity for patience, we reach for the round toys, and Nana scolds. She picks up the rolling pin.

The doughballs will suffer a pounding. Nana pushes and pulls, and before us, what was once three dimensional is now flattened, deconstructed. Flat balls. Flat and round. Magic performed with that wooden spinner. Nana's lips purse. She instructs with a heavy hand. These doughballs will obey.

Their form holds to the table when my brother and I forget to sprinkle enough snow dust in the right places, and then Nana scolds again. These flat circles fill the round table, edge to edge, like circle ruffles drawn with chalk on new fabric, ready to be cut and sewn onto a new dress. She plucks her thimble from her pocket and pushes tiny circles into the center of each flattened doughball. Circles within circles within circles make me dizzy and I plead for the thimble, for some tangible stillness. Nana relents, as long as I can train my eye to cut out each thimble circle in the perfect center. Like a pupil in iris. I aim and push. The tiny circles are removed and collected for a final doughball that we are allowed to practice on. When each of us rolls out a circle that looks more like an amoeba from my science textbook, Nana pulls it from the table and warms it in her palms again. She makes the amoeba back into a doughball, and we try the pin on it again before she takes it back once more. The doughball is born again, and again.

Nana places each flattened doughball into the hot oil and it bubbles and browns. She lifts them out of anointing with tongs, like extensions of her long fingernails, and lines them up on a paper towel–lined tin. There, she calls them buñuelos. Hot oil drips from each crisp and soaks the pink-dyed flowers on the paper towels to a bright fuchsia.

From a small pot on the back burner, Nana pours liquid-hot, cinnamon-infused piloncillo into repurposed jelly or olive jars. The table is wiped down again. The winter playground is gone, and we are once more in the desert, low and dry. She lines woven baskets with paper plates, and my brother and I sit practicing patience again.

Nana places the buñuelos on our plates and drizzles them with the dark-brown piloncillo syrup. Washed hands pick up the thin rounds and we move the disks from plate to palate. This one special buñuelo is allowed days before Christmas when Nana covers tins filled with dozens and delivers them to all the tíos and tías, Tata driving her in circles around Barrio Menlo.

Insatiable

That was it. Two slices of bread with mayo: a BLT without the bacon, without the lettuce, or tomato. That's all I got. We were poor, you know what I mean? I was always hungry, so when there was a party, there was no stopping me! I was first in line for the food. I was like an animal eating. I was always starving, my father says. I am in the Molino when I hear his hunger the loudest. I smell hunger on his breath. It is an emptiness I feel when I am surrounded by his pots and bottles and bowls brimming.

FIGURE 8 Tony Peyron in front of Tata's truck in the 1940s. Photo from author's personal collection.

you are not what you eat

but when you eat
touch hands to lips
and tongue to fingers
let your licks be
shameless
undefiled
when summoning
words
from heart
to throat
through teeth
let words be
pruned or all
together rooted up
don't let the unplanted
come out
your mouth
those slanders
and seeds of all
foul
feeding
will eat you
from the
inside out

—*el pensamiento*

Nopal Graffiti

Ricky and I sat beneath Nana's oak tree picking up the bellotas that fell to the ground, cracking them between our teeth like Nana taught us, and eating them, their bitter flavor mixed with a salt dust coating their shells. When we were full, or tired of this precious work, we wandered in Nana's garden.

I picked up a stick, a twig like a snake from under the carport shade, and I waved it in the air, as children often do, and I walked to the eastern edge of Nana's garden, pressing whatever boundary I could. I passed weed grass and the graveled area next to Tata's cuartito. I came to the low chain link fence at the alley, where there was a large patch of nopales growing tall in the rising sun, and I touched my stick snake to the center of a nopal leaf, marking its skin. The succulent leaves were thornless and tender, and the dark impressions I painted exposed wet flesh. I drew jagged lines and crisscrosses that devoured an entire leaf.

I wanted more, so I moved on to another leaf pad, and another, drawing out different shapes and testing pressure points that pleased me, then bored me until I retreated indoors to watch cartoons with Ricky.

Nana's voice came from the garden as she entered the side door through her kitchen. She called, *Where are you?!* She called to me, *Mijita, what have you done?*

At once, I realized I'd left my stick snake in the gravel, a succulent slime still green on its end. But in the admonishing, I failed to understand why this nopal tree mattered at all. I questioned: Had Nana even planted this tree and was anything part of the garden if it lived in the alley, on the border of our world, not even visible from the back porch? Was it even hers, I questioned, and how could a plant accompanied by only a rugged saguaro and rocks and empty bellota shells scattering in the wind matter to her?

I never saw the nopales admired or watered or mentioned before or after that day, though the marks I made on its pads were deep and remained for many months, maybe years. My questions went unanswered, yet a shame lived on in me and stung long past my days in Nana's garden.

Quick

I went to Catholic school on the right side of town, where I'd learn what must be the opposite of corn and fire and hands in manteca. Sometimes at school, during morning Mass or in religion class, I'd hear a lesson about eating, cooking, or meals in the Bible. There were many things I was supposed to know, like the time Abraham invited God to have a meal with him and so Abraham told his wife, Sarah, *Quick. Make bread.* I didn't understand the point of the story and, anyway, I'd forgotten all the parts to it, but there were times when the stories would overlap with Molino materiality, where they'd fold over each other like two sides of a desert border. A kind of kitchen déjà vu.

I remember *quick.* It was a customer's voice. It was my father's repeating. It was the picture of food in my mind. Food in numbers. Fast. When I stopped writing down customers' orders and started memorizing instead, I felt free. I didn't have to hold a pen and paper. I didn't have to worry about how food was spelled. I didn't have to reach into my apron pocket over and over. I could see names and plates of food in my mind. I could separate orders like street signs, like times tables, like faces: *beef-and-cheese burrito; chicken taco salad; one red tamale and a cup of beans.*

These words were spoken to me over and over in various combinations, unremitting like faith statements. And I packed them into my head rather than my notebook as they were spoken to me over the top of a glass deli case, a refrigerator the width of the storefront separating the Molino's inside from the big outside world. I held words in my hands and in my mouth in the kitchen. I folded and I ladled. Scooped and sprinkled. I put things together. I tried to make them pretty. I arranged chips, cheese, lettuce, and tomatoes in a circle. Black olives dotted plates like pinacate beetles.

Salsa cups spilled over onto my fingers. I wrapped with wax paper and moved quickly. I presented small paper bags of tamales and tall cups of iced cold cinnamon tea with plastic lids and straws. I placed everything in its place. My fingers tapped a register like piano keys. Tiny beeps filled the room. Quick notes. Quick tones. Bell warnings hastened everyone's steps.

NOW! my father chanted. Now was the time. Now was the moment to be seized. The moment to be a server who would impress. A servant who skillfully moved, making no mistakes, and moving fast like the hands of a man chopping meat at the taqueria. Hands like machines. Eyes like beams of light focused on a grill. Quick.

In the Molino I was busy, never still. Hearing God's voice in the middle of being busy would have made me laugh like Sarah, like water splashing. Dough and water and butter spread thin on my mind. Sarah kneaded. I folded. God waited for us beneath a tree, squatting on a concrete curb, pulling our food apart in his mouth, like thunder and lightning. *Where is Sarah?* He asked.

Where is that girl with brown eyes? The one who smells like me? He asks. *She needs to slow down. Not so quick. Be still.*

Is anything too hard for the Lord?

Killing

It is hot in the kitchen when I arrive. I pull the apron over my head, tying it around my expanding waist. I rub my hands together under water at the small sink station. I greet everyone, *Good morning.* I'm polite and short and pretend to be a good girl in the Molino.

I line up tomatoes and set a serrated knife down on the cold stainless steel. My cutting board is slashed and stained. The top layer of its plastic is shredded and feathering with age. It has been here a while, and who knows how long it will remain. I roll one tomato out into the center of the board. I slice it in half and yellow seeds spill out. They swim in a shallow lake of pink liquid and get pushed to the side. I slice again and again and the chopped pieces get dumped into a plastic bin that will fit perfectly into its spot in the deli case.

Ricky is beside me. He is cutting green onions and talking and talking about something or nothing. He is wielding a long, serrated knife, and I carry its twin in my right hand when we begin to raise our voices at each other in anger.

Who knows what this is about.

Probably Ricky is making fun of me. Probably I am criticizing him. I am irritated, overheated and prepubescent. He is trapped, bored, and rough. Our shouting match soon fills every inch of the kitchen, and when my father has had enough, he comes to scold us.

He will tell the story to everyone for the rest of the day. He will even tell my nana and tata and they will look at me until I shrivel.

They were trying to kill each other! he'll say, and everyone will gasp and shake their heads.

What were they thinking? he'll ask.

He won't mention he is the one putting knives in our hands, the one setting us before all the things we can't escape: cases of tomatoes, green onions, green chiles, and cheese with no end in sight. These weapons are slow, but not harmless. They are like heavy blankets that drive you mad. Like bowls of beans, familiar and comfortable and bottomless.

Barbacoa Pit

Though I felt like I spent half my childhood in my tata's backyard, I don't remember his barbacoa pit. My father says it was next to the cuartito, Tata's small tool shed, at the back of his yard where the nopales grew in Barrio Menlo. I must have walked over the pit a thousand times, never realizing I was hovering over a deep hole in the earth. I wondered how I could miss something so big and hollow. I watched my tata eat a cut of beef almost every day, but I have no memory of the barbacoa pit. He had left the ranch for the city of Tucson a long time before, but his customs were set, and the cattle were never far from his plate.

My father wanted to serve barbacoa at the Molino and at catered weddings, so he dug a deep hole in our backyard too. It was Holy Week when my mother's cousins came from San Diego to Tucson for Easter, and Cousin Rogelio helped my father chisel through the caliche while the rest of the family flew kites over the desert behind the house. The hole was carved slowly from Palm Sunday through Good Friday. When it was done, my father lined it with two layers of oven bricks and mortar, then placed metal doors over the top.

To cook the barbacoa, my father opened the doors and set a fire with mesquite wood collected from the desert on the other side of our patio wall. He anointed beef with garlic, oregano, and salt and placed it in tinas, large metal tubs that could withstand the fire. The enormous pots had to be lowered with at least two strong sets of arms—each person standing at the top of the pit, clasping rods my father fashioned with large wire hooks on one end and pot handles on the other. Lowered carefully, a pot might suspend over the embers for a weighted minute before it finally touched the bottom of the pit. I remember the grimaces of that labor. The weight on those poles pulled at backs, shoulders, and footholds like a flash flood of meat and muscle. Everything seemed to contract over the flame and smoke.

My father never dropped a pot. Not once. Ricky was often the brawn opposite him over the pit, but my father never asked me to do this job with him. I watched. The metal doors closed over the pit and the whole thing was buried in earth. My brother and I pushed mud and dirt into the holes between the bricks around the pit. Wherever smoke seeped out of the mortar, we pressed in with pebbles and wet dirt, a desert clay, to seal the earthen oven. I remember feeling the heat off those bricks as we circled around the pit in procession. I remember the smell starting there in the yard and eventually making its way into our house, its smoldering and bubbling air seeping in through the swamp cooler and the cracks in doorframes. For days, the coyotes and mountain lion could smell my father's barbacoa wafting through the desert. Smoke lingered, staining our hair and clothes and bed linens—an odor that signaled a softening and submission, the smell of shredded flesh, meat moistened, infused, and falling from the bone.

Bodas de Barbacoa

My forehead holds small beads of sweat and I stand by long folding tables covered in bright-colored zarapes. Large stainless steel chafing dishes hover over small fuel cans radiating a blue flame. We are at the Knights of Columbus, or the American Legion, or El Casino Ballroom. I forget which. There is the smell of hair spray, wet cigarettes, bleached linoleum floors. This is El Rapido's buffet-style catered wedding.

The bride and groom have chosen this food, my father's food, for one of the most important days of their lives. He will serve barbacoa, seasoned and shredded beef that has been simmered slowly overnight in our backyard pit. There is rice, green pea–sprinkled and peach-tinted with a bottle of Knorr brand Caldo de Tomate con Sabor de Pollo. Beans are pinto and pork-laced. Salsa de chile verde, a condiment that can become the main course when rolled in a flour tortilla while running late to work, is a compilation of salted rajas, white onions, tomatoes, and cilantro all swimming together in a bowl at the end of the table like my father's signature at the bottom of a certificate. Tortillas de harina, still warm from Anita Street Market or Alejandro's Tortilla Factory on South Twelfth Avenue, have been special ordered for this boda de barbacoa.

I'm twelve years old.

My father yells to me from the banquet room where the reception has already begun. *Bring me more spoons! Nooowww! And take those tortillas out of the bag. And start fanning those napkins out on the table . . .* His orders ring out like a to-do list written in red ink.

Well, which do you want me to do? I scream back in frustration. *Spoons!*

Spoons, tongs, and ladles lie around in abundance, but somehow, there are never enough, so I hurry back into the small kitchen. I scour through Tucson Fruit and Produce cardboard boxes that hold everything my father owns today— matches, calculator, wilted business cards, plastic forks, containers with no matching lids, lids with no matching containers, a lone corn tortilla chip. These items can only be found easily if you have a good memory, or a healthy sense of adventure. My father doesn't remember much from before last week, but he can find almost every misplaced thing he owns. He knows the not-so-great place to keep things. For him, the wrong place becomes the perfect place for an unfound object. It is more exciting that way. It is a riddle. Something to consider on long car drives. It is an anecdote at holiday parties. Like when you reach into your old coat pocket and find, among old tissue paper and pennies, a perfectly crisp five-dollar bill. That joy in finding the one thing you hadn't realized you had with you the whole time will propel you to start searching in every wrong place for the right thing.

I can't find it! I complain, in front of wedding guests.

Look around, he says for the three-thousandth time in my life. *Look around! Look around!* As though things were meant to be found by accident.

The bride is wearing white poof. Creamy, satiny, and sweaty. She and I are strangers. I don't know her skin. I don't know her voice. The Knights of Columbus is the only place we ever cross paths, and all I can know of her is this day and how she moves between people and plastic chairs like a gliding white light. The gown she wears is like all the others at every other catered wedding on every other weekend. Too poofy for me. And besides, at twelve, I am not getting married. Not ever. I'm not meant for it. This I'm sure of. I'm sure the boys who want me only want me because I am big chested. My breasts are a gift but not a blessing, a branding of the woman I am not ready to become. I am awkward and growing sideways, like a bubble. I am not pretty.

Rather, I am slowly becoming what I'm convinced is shameful to look at. Vulgar even. My bubbling means I am always *getting* fat. It's a trajectory I can't seem to avoid. Someday I will have *gotten* fat, so I've started hunching over in an attempt to begin canceling the flesh that is not beautiful. Twelve years old does not feel beautiful to me. Other twelve-year-old things like wanting attention from boys may be understandable, but they are hopeless. Because twelve years old, itself, feels hopeless. It is disappointments, realizations, failures, and bubbling breasts. At twelve, there is only one thing I crave more than love with a boy. It is a wanting to evacuate my body. It is a desire to be outside of me. A desire to float away.

In an apron, I look matronly, so wedding guests ask me for my "husband" when they mean my father. Am I my brother's mother? Ricky never seems to have to answer to anyone, I think. It seems to me that he is allowed to be a child even into adulthood. He reclines in a chair at the end of the buffet line, waiting on us, and looking like a miniature football player after a game. His worn sneakers swing back and forth beneath ashy knees. From behind, he looks like my father. My father barks at him, and Ricky snickers back like spitting water, then he finally takes his spot at the serving line. The three of us stand side by side, looking related and annoyed. My mother is never here.

My father flings a plate at me, and I stand up straight. The hierarchy goes like this: my hyper father first serving the barbacoa, me in the center serving beans and rice, dimpled Ricky at the end with salsa and tortillas. This hierarchy is visually clear in tallest to shortest, but I've stopped growing taller, so Ricky will pass my persistent five-feet height soon. Since I'm older, I'll always be before salsa. Although this hierarchy of main entrée, side dishes, and condiments in concordance with Molino seniority is never verbally discussed, it makes its way into every catering job. I feel as though I am born in front of beans and rice. It is my God-given purpose and my birthright.

Wedding guests hover, floating closer and closer to our table, impatient for the bride and groom, who are supposed to be served first. When white poof finally arrives, the bride looks overjoyed at the buffet line, as though she weren't actually paying us to feed her. I am ready with rice in spoon, spoon in right hand, left hand ready for the plate handoff. I serve without looking anyone in the eye. I see flashes of white poof. My eyes are fixated on plates, portions, and my own wrist rotations, dipping, scooping, pouring. Only split seconds are available to brush hands along aprons when necessary. I listen only momentarily to special instructions: *I am a vegetarian . . . I need two servings of this . . . None of that, thank you.*

The three of us together serve three hundred people in thirty minutes or less, $4.50 a plate for friends and family, more for the general public. The profit is enough for water bills, gas bills, and whatever Ricky and I want from the mall that weekend, but we are easily pleased: video games, costume jewelry, movie tickets, and ice-cream cones do it for us. *Disposable income*, it is called. It is a ridiculous and disrespectful term I imagine makes my great-grandparents roll over in their graves. Though I know the value of this money, I'm a kid. Kids and money, as a pair, don't last long.

As we break down the buffet and wait to pick up empty plates, a DJ orchestrates white poof and tuxedos. He is a teenage boy, probably a cousin of somebody, and I immediately crave and simultaneously fear his attention. Dressed all in black, and wearing a hat and sunglasses indoors, this strobe light–toting boy makes me hate my place in front of steaming food. I hide behind kitchen doors so he won't see me greñuda, sweaty, carrying awkward breasts under a dirty apron, serving rice and beans. I pray to be the ignored kitchen-helping daughter of the barbacoyero. From afar, I watch him hold a mic and spin. I look for his face beneath his hat, and his music plays loud and fills everyone with a tremor.

I listen while I clean, wipe, lift, load. I work while lights flash on the dance floor. In my listening, I find myself serving like my father until the DJ's song about freedom teases wonder from me, like a new flavor on my tongue. Somewhere in the song, someone calls me. I hear my name. Not the name my mother calls me or my father calls me. Not a name I've been called before, but still one that sounds like me. I remember I am dying to escape the heated room of the kitchen in which I live. Soon the DJ's undeniable melody gives a pinhole view of new days ahead, however incomplete, and the view makes me want to fly off the ground and land somewhere else. Like Dorothy moving from black and white to color.

I work, but the music plays louder. It begins to float me, then I decide. I don't care who sees me. I don't care what price I might have to pay, what my father will say, what the bride in poof will think. I simply stop in my tracks and turn. I walk onto the crowded parquet floor, between the bodies there in motion under lights, and I start to dance with them. Hard. In apron. Until the song stops.

on the wall

I sleep at the end
of rebozo fringe
between lands you never knew were touching
those color wheel peripheries
I am the space between cream and coffee
the before the after primordial puntas y picachos
santa ritas my tumamoc my cat mountain overlapping
a west-side sunset cradling you

can you see my skin
between the palos verdes

when the ride takes you east and you squint into sunrise
cast your gaze upward above the uprooted
horizontal saguaro
waving from truck trailers
up to the rivers running above all this dirt they call
from one brink to another
el pueblo viejo

—*el pensamiento*

Sunday Clothes

I am wearing cutoffs or a miniskirt, something stained. Mama says, *You can't wear that to church.* My shape makes everyone in the room uncomfortable and doubtful. I've failed at another diet, and my skin peaks through threads, rolls out over edges, breaches every border.

I talk back to Mama. My tongue licks the layers between us. *God doesn't care what I wear* is what I say, as though God never imagined lambs' wool or garment hems, as though God can't weave and isn't in the habit of caring. Mama doesn't have a good answer for this, as far as I am concerned. She hovers in the doorway, a storm over her own skin ballooning into midlife, besieged by half my wardrobe blanketing royal-blue carpet, a few layers thick. A weak barrier between us. There we tangle in the cords and cottons, both of us needing a Sabbath's rest from this.

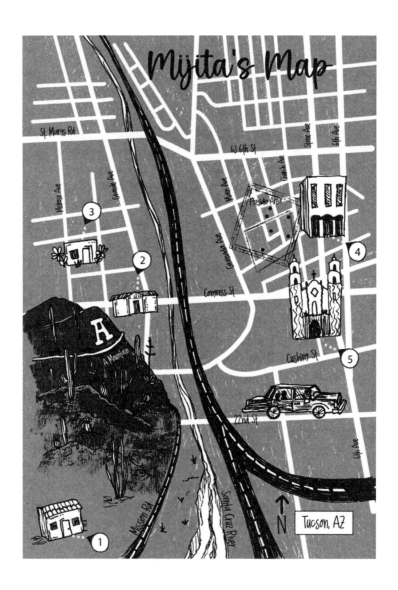

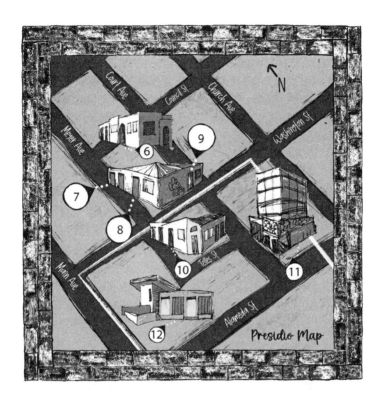

Presidio Map

1 Mijita's home
2 Aurelio & Martina's Menlo home
3 Nana & Tata's Menlo home
4 Mountain Bell building
5 St. Augustine's Cathedral
6 The Stork's Nest
7 Juanita's Beauty Shop
8 Perez Presidio home
   (original El Rapido storefront)
9 El Rapido
10 Old Town Artisans
11 Transamerica building
12 Tucson Museum of Art

Maps by Alex Jimenez

Our Mother of Sorrows

When we reached junior high, Ricky and I rode the public bus forty-five minutes each way to Our Mother of Sorrows Catholic School. After early mornings at the Molino, we took the number 4 bus from the downtown Ronstadt Transit Center on Sixth Avenue. It carried us east on Speedway Boulevard past the University of Arizona, turned south on Kolb Road, and dropped us on a corner in front of our school in a community that was thirteen miles from our home. From what I could tell, my father never wanted us to go there, but my mother insisted.

None of my schoolmates lived on our side of town, and perhaps my father knew this would become a problem. For him, the east side was another planet. Many of my schoolmates had never been to downtown Tucson, much less to our Molino. Most of them were middle to upper class, and though I never asked, I was sure none of them worked in tamal or tortilla factories.

My mother had also attended Our Mother of Sorrows school and church. Her mother had also insisted. My maternal grandmother made sure to move her family to the east side of Tucson when they had come from Southern California in the 1950s, as my grandfather had taken a job as a mechanic with the Southern Pacific Railroad. This decision ensured my mother would grow up in a neighborhood, not a barrio. Dogs would be leashed. Dinners would be roast beef, broccoli, and boxed macaroni and cheese.

But not everything from Baja could be left behind. I imagine the other kids at Our Mother of Sorrows noticed the difference between themselves and my mother. She ate peanut butter or jelly on tortillas. She ate smashed beans on Wonder Bread. I imagine this was not an easy thing to explain. She was the only one with a Spanish surname, the only one whose parents spoke Spanish at home. This couldn't be an easy thing to explain. She denies needing to explain anything. She was just like the other kids, she says. She thought Ricky and I would be too. So that we'd be spared tamalero futures, she and my grandmother paid Catholic school tuition for fourteen years straight.

Hope grew, even as my mother must have questioned our school-delivered motivations of *Hard work pays off* or *Anything is possible if you put your mind to it* or those expectations of prosperity and privilege. Hope waded through the sacrifice of monthly tuition payments and forty-five-minute bus rides and being teased for not looking Mexican enough nor eating American enough, along with a deep sense of being from another planet. Hope itself called these strange ingredients, a good mix of fortune and sacrifice, to transform, under fire, or by miraculous chemical reaction, into children free from sorrows. The kind of sorrows mothers and fathers had flowing in their veins. The kind of sorrows that swelled on long bus rides or in empty bank accounts. Sorrows that only mothers recognized, and only mothers could prevent.

Lincoln Town Car

Though my mother protested, my father bought our used 1987 Lincoln Town Car from Uncle Mike. It had power locks and power windows on little chrome levers. Wood paneling framed its dark-blue velour interior. There was a radio antenna integrated into the rear window glass, and sometimes I traced its thin brown lines with my fingers on long drives. The Lincoln Town Car was a gas glutton.

Each day, we wielded the Town Car down the hill of our drive-way, a descent from our home in Paradise Mountain Estates—the collection of permanent and mobile homes in a place people now call the "west foothills." We never called our neighborhood by those names. *Estates* is a word we didn't own. *Foothills* is a word that means a place for people we probably didn't know—people literally living in higher places. My family never put ourselves in those clubs, but Dad's Lincoln Town Car purchase may have been an attempt at getting closer to class. I thought of that silly car as our own personal dirt-and-dust-covered limo. We lived on a dirt road and the dust could never be fully erased from either interior or exterior. But sometimes dirt roads transform into semi-elite places. Unlike neighborhoods "in the city," a lack of smooth side-walks meant no place for drunks to comfortably pass out in front of our house.

Against the dirt, the Lincoln shined like gold. It told everyone Tony had sold enough tamales and tortillas to live large. It was an American dream, even patriotic. It was a used car, but it was luxury, like a cruise ship on its last voyage. Since my father needed a truck for work, my mom had to wrestle the boxy boat down the mountain to work every day. Its bow dodged jackrabbits. The stern bounced on rattlesnake speed bumps. My mother in the hull sunk herself into plush bench seats, playing the radio all the way from paradise to downtown Tucson. She steered east on Congress, then north on Sixth Avenue to Alameda Street to a final destination at the Mountain Bell–turned–AT&T building, where she sat before a switchboard and listened to people over wires for eleven dollars an hour. I don't remember my father ever driving the Lincoln Town Car, the vehicle he had insisted should be the *family* car.

On Christmas Eve 1991, after our usual tamal dinner at Uncle Mike's, my mother carried us in the Lincoln Town Car to midnight Mass on the opposite side of town. We sailed from west to east so many times, in every family car we owned. We crossed the railroad tracks so often, the bounce of wheels on railroad tracks and ties were as familiar as heartbeats. This transition was more of a tradition than midnight Mass would ever be for us. We all knew the movement, this journey from pole to pole, as common as sunrise and sunset.

The year 1991 had been a tough one. I was thirteen years old. Ricky was a middle-school late bloomer. My mother was watching her mother live through one last year of the cancer that would take her. My father was starting to hang out with other families instead of ours. There were many other reasons to eat and eat until I was overflowing. Still, there was at least one Christmas miracle: my father agreeing to go to midnight Mass with us at Our Mother of Sorrows church. It was an added miracle that he would stay awake, since the hours after 5:00 p.m. on Christmas Eve were those sweet, slippery times of leisure and excess and exhaustion—my father's hours after a long last day of Christmas tamal season at the Molino. He hardly spoke, mumbling only some complaints of the cold and grunting in response to questions.

I remember Monsignor Calahan in his holiday robe standing tall and center at the church altar. I remember carpets lined in red-and-white cuetlaxochitl, la flor de Nochebuena, leading the way to a nativity scene. The sanctuary was lit by candles, casting shadows on squirming children whose mocos leaked all over their special Christmas costumes. This would be a long and drawn-out ritual—with a few extra repetitions of the chorus, with extended pomp. Somehow these amplifications and expansions would communicate that everyone was glad for Our Savior's birth. But I wasn't sure. I hadn't been convinced that any of this drama pleased a baby born in a manger. I had no interest in babies or gods posing as babies or babies posing as gods, so I sat sleepily between my mother and Ricky on the pew of a stuffy sanctuary. I don't remember where my father sat, but I remember his eyes closed throughout the mass.

Between the responsorial psalm and the gospel acclamation, Ricky leaned across me and whispered to my mother that he was feeling sick and needed to lie down. I saw her teeth grinding in anger, but what could she do? Fuss in the middle of midnight Mass? Argue in front of the nativity scene? Our mother of sorrows was forced to let Ricky go sleep in the car, with no grilling for explanation or proof. My brother walked out of the church in the middle of the night alone and passed out in the Lincoln Town Car while the rest of us went through the motions of midnight Mass in drowsy unison.

I was jealous, of course. And I was sure my mother had been fooled.

I imagined my brother settling into that soft bench seat of the Lincoln Town Car, dreaming. I imagined him slipping away in deep, free rest. My arms folded in church, my ears closed to the prayers being said, my nose upturned to body and blood. I didn't sing along with the joyful songs coming from the congregation. Mine were the hollow handshakes and shallow kisses of peace. My ignoring was my only escape, like a daydream woven in resentment. I imagined my years of misery while Ricky dove headfirst into pleasure. I imagined the older sibling in a parable—the one about excess and fanfare and parties and pleasure all laid at the feet of the wayward son—an elder sibling fuming and sweeping away any mention of grace or blessing or stories of birth and salvation.

I was sick too. Because I didn't want to go back and forth from west to east. Because my parents didn't like each other and never kissed outside of the sign of peace at Mass. Because Christmas costumes were uncomfortable, and tías commenting on costumes were worse. Because I didn't want to ride around in a Lincoln Town Car and pretend.

After Mass, we found Ricky asleep in the back seat. I had no sympathy. My father fell into the front passenger seat and my mother drove us home. We were a few hundred yards from Our Mother of Sorrows when Ricky woke up, sat up, and said he felt sick. Even though the car was moving, in the 2:00 a.m. darkness of the back seat, I heard the click of the door handle. I heard Ricky trying to open the door while my mother drifted us down the road. He clawed at the window and door locks, but they were all locked and childproof. That is when Ricky's half-digested dinner of red chile Christmas tamales spewed all over the back seat of my father's prized Lincoln Town Car.

We all jerked in surprise. The boat rocked a bit. I turned away and put my hands over my mouth and nose, but the sound was as bad as the smell. Ricky kept vomiting while my mother continued to drive, repeating *It's OK, Ricky, you'll be all right* in the same kind of voice she used at work over the telephone wires, patient and friendly. She probably reached to the back seat to put a comforting hand on my brother, but the town car was too big, the expanse from interior front to back and side to side too wide between us for solace. My father, disgusted, never looked at Ricky or said a word. He immediately rolled down his window only to realize the rush of winter night air was too cold for him to handle. He proceeded to maneuver the window up and down, and I could hear the power lever being flicked and forced by his sluggish grip. Up and down. Up and down. Up to keep the cold out, down to let the smell out. Finally, he cracked the window about two inches from the top. By this time, the smell of red chile and ground-up corn and whatever else was on my aunt Carmen's Christmas Eve dining table that night mixed with Ricky's gastric juices penetrated every inch of the hull. Man overboard. So my father sat up tall and reached his nose and mouth to the tiny crack in the car window. He sucked in cold air and exhaled the kind of groan you hear in movies when everyone is puking. Guttural, but dry. His lips poked out of the crack in the window as he made these vomiting noises like a drunken transient. Like a character in a movie. But not *The Exorcist*. More like *Stand by Me*. Or *The Goonies*, the movies that are as scary as horror flicks when you don't even realize it. My father was like the lead role in those movies.

As my mother pulled the Lincoln Town Car back to shore, I stared at him, my father, not my brother. I was dumbfounded. He wasn't even in the back seat with the worst of it. It was the most exaggerated case of empathic nausea I'd ever listened to. That is when I finally felt pity for my brother. He was truly sick and I was sitting in the proof. When we got out of the car, my father ran into the house, still gagging, and I don't remember seeing him for the rest of the night. My mother helped Ricky into bed, then she and I walked out to the Lincoln Town Car, holding buckets of soapy water and rolls of paper towels.

My family never forgets the time we sat together in the Lincoln Town Car on Christmas Eve in 1991. I suppose lots of people never forget things that happen on holy days. Remembering is like an anchor at the bottom of an ocean. If it holds on, it manifests holiness. I forget so many things, but I can't forget smelling what came out of us that night. My eyes still see the color of it. I remember looking at my mother and cringing as we wiped it all up under a Christmas-morning sky of stars and moon. We didn't say much, but in disgust I finally blurted out, *How can you do this?* And I remember her saying, *This is what mothers do, mijita.*

Crossing

Ricky and I were driven to the east side of town and without saying it, that driving meant somehow the east side was smarter than the west, which I became confused by; it was a thing I didn't know how to say or how to ask. All I knew was this crossing back and forth, on a bus or in my father's truck, was meant to bring us to a better place.

We crossed the bridge over empty washes and railroad tracks, booze parks on one side and zoo animals on the other. We crossed overpasses both ways, like an upward mobility, a downhill summer—west to east, east to west, all to drive some things out of us and to drive other things in. When we got eighth grade done at Our Mother of Sorrows, a piece of paper proved we had surpassed our ancestors.

What I learned in school had me wondering if nanas and tatas knew what I knew, and if not, why what they knew seemed small enough to fit in a pot on the stove.

Not all of them finished eighth grade like me, like Ricky. They were never school dress coded in the right colors, penny loafering like us. And that difference between us meant I didn't realize I had already begun asking painful questions of my ancestors, over cups of coffee or by a stovetop flame. Beside gutted catfish, under lines of laundry baked in their backyards, I grilled my grandparents.

How far did you go in school? I asked. Sometimes their answers were single digits. The numbers smoked or seared, like a branding or like the wrong answers on a Scantron test. The numbers were inked like lottery tickets worth nothing more than hope in a pocket of a housecoat or a pair of Levi's.

That is just the way it was, they'd say. *In those days, we had to quit school and start working, mijita. There was no choice.*

I'd feel their voices sink down into the ground. I imagined a void spreading somewhere on an unsigned document packed away with photos and newspaper clippings, sifted to the bottom of the back bedroom cajón. I imagined scrapbooks made of scraps instead of certificates with the words the world wants, words written down.

But I was lucky. Someone paid for my Catholic school tuition, my white lace gowns, gold cross pendants, and embossed prayer books. Money, they say, is a money thing. Tú sabes. Money meant I graduated from eighth grade. I have the papers to prove it. I have the pictures too: I'm surrounded by smiling familia, their hands on my shoulders, greeting cards poking out of their purses, a huddle of nanas and tatas looking proud in their Sunday best on my eighth-grade graduation day. They gave this to me—this finishing, this completion. It was them, my own lovely, loaded, full-to-the-brim nanas and tatas from both sides of a line we don't cross anymore. I want to hold their names in my pockets, signed in all curly cursive, and retrieve them to smooth out their lines and creases. Then, maybe someday, I will understand why I'd be so confused by all the things small enough to fit in a pot on the stove.

PART IV

a tortilladora

casting hot iron
black against a wall
a metallic villain a conveyor
laboring hot slop everclear beginning
middle and end
a finishing of round anonymous
tortillas ascend a tower
a toasting a snowfall
a maize luster full
moons slipping like infants her brown eyes
cocoons kernels little
balls of dough electrified sparrows
the other side of sodden windows palm leaf crosses
a flat earth swaddle
a fire belt rapture assembled
on gears an industrial memory
a moloch mechanical sheol
eternal making elbow
wrist and knuckle
dipped in apron pocket
burned and buried

—*el pensamiento*

Burned

Surrounded by desert, my city was lifted out of the caliche. Skirted by mountains on all sides, Tucson is 227 square miles, but my home inside this ring of dirt and cacti and dry riverbeds is the one square mile of downtown Tucson, a few streets of structures and heartbeats huddled together. Cars and bikes and pedestrians do not buzz here. They spin. They coil around ancient adobe walls paired with modern curtain wall constructions. They lean on white lines and black lines that tangle, then roll out into the four sacred corners. Here, thorns grow in the cracks. Here, asphalt and brick pull up to nopales and flat land reaches up with stairsteps and elevator shafts. Our towering buildings are not sky rises and can't compete with the mountaintops.

My father was born here before the buildings blocked mountain views. On Court Avenue north of Washington, the Stork's Nest maternity ward brought him into the Presidio—Tucson's Spanish fortress. He was named Antonio Perez Peyron and laid in a crib a block away, in a one-room apartment with saguaro-ribbed ceilings. That room now holds silver and turquoise, pottery and weavings for sale to tourists at Old Town Artisans. Across Washington Street is the house where my grandmother grew up—the three-room home for a family of eleven. Today Washington Street begins west at Main and ends east at the YMCA on Church Avenue. I can reach one end to the other in 388 steps.

Almost no one lives in this neighborhood anymore. Grocery stores are replaced with law firms. Department stores are replaced by offices. Some banks remain, like old men who refuse to retire. Around this corner or that, settlers lean back into office chairs, slide across dining booths, or balance on barstools. My family still weaves in and out of downtown.

Near the corner of Alameda Street and Scott Avenue, my mother worked as a telephone operator two flights up in the Mountain Bell building. My brother rode his bike seconds away, usually somewhere between City Court and the abandoned Fox Theatre. My father spun himself around his kitchen, and I was often his messenger of burros, fajitas, tamales, red chile, chorizo, machaca, frijoles, and tortillas. On his errands, I paced Alameda and Church all summer long.

I remember thinking it strange that my mother and father wouldn't let my brother and I stay out too late, wouldn't take us to México, and wouldn't let us go to public school, but we were allowed to be walking alone downtown, carrying a paper bag of food in one hand and a wad of money in the other. We were not monitored in alleyways, in parking garages, or in cement corridors. The summer sun was oppressive on our deliveries, but we lived some independence on downtown streets. We most often walked or cycled alone. We didn't wear headphones or carry cell phones. We circled around in that space and were left to our own thoughts, which, if we wanted, could take us far away.

My daydreams, like a mirage, were blurred by desert heat. The sun made me tired, angry, and delusional. I'd open the side-gate exit from the kitchen, step out onto Washington, and melt into tar pavement. The sun would bake me from above, and the cement sidewalk would grill me from below. A few yards like this, and I was on fire. The sunny side of streets was vacant as those afoot trafficked the shady walkways, their routes changing with the sundial. My delivery time was dependent on sunrays. I took shortcuts—to cool my route rather than actually shorten it. I'd diagonal through air-conditioned lobbies, cut through misted patios, rest under canopies or statues. Under the mosaic-tiled Pima County courthouse dome, I took refuge. By its pillars, I wiped my brow with my T-shirt. Many times, I stood motionless at the entrance of the main library, its cool air licking me each time someone entered and exited. Bank foyers, office reception rooms, elevators, stairways—they were my sanctuaries. Upon return to the steamed air of El Rapido, I dove head and shoulders into the industrial kitchen refrigerator or deli case, until my father's reprimand found me and I had to shut the doors to cool, crisp air.

When I wasn't familiar with the delivery address, my father scribbled maps and directions on wax paper wrappers and number 4 brown paper bags. His handwriting was like a series of personal signatures. The first three letters of words could be deciphered, but the rest trailed off into illegible loops and strings. He saw my confusion and pointed different directions impatiently, invisible destinations implied beyond his curved and crooked index finger. He started with reference points I wasn't sure of.

Go to 210 West Congress, make a left at the bus stop, and go up the stairs. It's right there, he urged.

Which one is 210? I asked, not knowing even where to begin. There was no "You Are Here" sticker on his maps. I was often lost. I reached many of my destinations by bumping into them.

I stood at the wrought iron door of El Rapido, peering, dazed at his blue ink on white parchment, and his impatience would swell into sarcastic barks: *LEFT. RIGHT. UP. DOWN.* Then finally a surrender: *If you get lost, just look for the mountains, and then you'll know which way is north*, he said. Though layered ranges of mountains encircled all of Tucson, he was serious.

The best deliveries were the close ones. The closest were literally steps away—either at the Tucson Museum of Art around the corner or at a jewelry vendor across the street at Old Town Artisans. Old Town was a favorite. As children, my brother and I loved delivering there. Blessed by the tour through silver and clay home adornments, wildlife postcards, and billowing peasant blouses, our run was usually capped off with a generous tip for two minutes' work. We often delivered to a silversmith there, an older and friendly man, short with a round belly. He liked my father's red chile and root beer. After delivering his burrito and extra-large cup filled with crushed ice, he'd let us watch him at his stonecutter as he fashioned textured rings, jewel pendants, bolo ties, and earrings. He wore his black hair in a long braid that fell down the center of his back.

One Friday afternoon at the end of the workday, he found me returning from a bank errand in the parking garage passageway beneath the Transamerica building. He smiled and I smiled back. He spoke to me in a calm voice.

Where's your brother? I didn't see him today.

Oh, he already went back to school, I said.

What about you? Isn't your summer over yet?

It's my last day, I said smiling, *and Monday is my first day of high school.*

I was radiant. I was done wandering around this maze and ready to be with friends, to be in a new place, to be outside my urban detention. I was a pretty girl on that day, a few weeks into another diet to hide the rolls that seemed to grow around me. Even after a month of restrictive eating, I was full figured, and more like a woman. This teenage threshold made me glow, and the shine on me stretched out many inches from my skin.

Wow, that's great, congratulations, he said.

Thank you.

I'll miss you, he said as he stepped in and wrapped his arms around me.

He pulled me close without letting go, his face close to mine. He was speaking, but quieter, and I stopped hearing his words after that. I said nothing and only gripped the bank bag in my hand. I heard nothing. There was no car ignition, no squeal of wheels in the garage. No cars passed in the street, and no people or things walked, biked, jogged, or trickled by. I heard no children laughing like park fountains, and no transients dragging their words behind them like luggage. I heard nothing the jeweler was saying to me, and I stared down, casting my gaze on black pavement. My heartbeat met his, and his heavy arms bound me, sealed me in silver bracelets. I was calcified there in the shadows of concrete walls and steel piping, my glow eclipsed. I found myself unable to move or get away. Then he pulled me in hard to kiss me, and I jerked back against his chest. He slowly released his embrace and continued to speak through our tussle without a change in tone. Without disruption.

I'm so sad you'll be gone, he said, *but I bet you'll have fun in high school.*

I stood motionless, gawking at oil stains on that garage floor, but was otherwise polite to the jeweler. When he turned and casually said good-bye, I staggered out of the garage and into the sun. I walked back to the Molino.

My father had already locked up for the day. He was waiting for me in his pickup truck, parked the wrong direction on the one-way street, idling in front of the Sleepy Mexican. I scrambled into the truck, and the hot seat stung my bare legs. My father fidgeted with the small air-conditioning vents, trying to get as much air as possible, then gave up and rolled down the window. His hands searing on the black vinyl steering wheel, he drove us out of downtown. That's when the heat triggered chills on my skin—the body's self-preserving reaction, an onslaught of heat exhaustion.

I didn't know what I was feeling, exactly, but when a flood of tears came, I faced away from my father, gazing out the passenger window for the whole ride home. I don't know if he could hear my crying. I figured he either never noticed or never cared to ask me if I was OK. Together we sat in silence as the truck climbed the mountains home.

I never told. Not my mother, my father, nor my brother. Like steam, my memory of being trapped by the jeweler, his heavy breath on my lips, hung in the air over my head. Sometimes the thought of it seemed to shoot out of my fingertips, my eyes. For a long time, I would recoil, then petrify in the presence of most men.

There was no avoiding the garage under the Transamerica building after that summer. I still had to walk through it a thousand more times. I moved in and out of many of the corners and walkways of downtown. We all did. My mother moved carefully from the cool air of her office building to the heat of a blacktop parking lot and finally to a seat on the couch in front of our TV. Our summers marched by. My brother rode his bike down another street, and grew tired of selling tamales. The nineteen months between our birthdays seemed to expand further and further. My father spun around and around on the corner of Meyer and Washington. His voice grew louder as his sense of hearing faded away, and soon enough, he was deaf to us. For several years, we bumped and turned like a ride at the county fair, in the same tight space, smiling at each other, then scared, with more noises than words between us.

When I got my driver's license, I often escaped. Crossing the empty Santa Cruz River, I'd drive up to the top of Sentinel Peak—just three miles west and 250 feet up from the Presidio. There, up high on volcanic rock, I'd look below to the city, its miniature structures and microscopic movement, Transamerica like a stack of Legos. I'd sit quietly and sometimes I'd imagine all the teenage girls who got burned like me, some with deeper wounds than others. I'd think about the ones who don't tell. As I waited, the smell of creosote bush would fill my lungs. On the horizon I'd see dust clouds overtake the sun and cast the city in a pink blaze, a sepia-tone postcard. The thunderclouds followed, and soon the desert would be milled with late-summer monsoons that came to wash out the roasted earth and drench all of us who find ourselves on fire.

Espeak

¿No hables español? the customer says to me from the other side of the deli case. *¡Qué vergüenza! You work at a tamaleria, don't you? And you don't espeak Spanish?*

I listen as the words spin fast-forward in circles around me. I choke down my voice. I begin to wish my parents are here so I can point at them, so they can take the blame, but they'll only remember the teachers lining up little children in grade school bathrooms, their little mouths filled with Spanish, dirty words, soon to be washed out with soap. They'll taste the glycerin and foam. They won't say it out loud to me, but they will think it: *Spanish is not good for you, mijita.*

I got saved, you know that? my dad tells me. *When they lined us up in first grade at the soap dispenser, there was a boy in front of me. I think . . . maybe it was Dickie Carrillo or maybe it was Frankie Pesquiera. I can't remember. Anyway, he puked on the teacher. Man, the kids in line, we wanted to pick him up on our shoulders! He saved the day, man!* My dad raises his fists in victory. *Shoulda washed out the mouth of that butthole who did that to us,* he says, shaking his head. *But hey, me and everyone behind me? We were all saved.*

A few Spanish-speaking customers will walk out the door on me, in frustration. In disbelief. I won't be able to talk about it. I won't be able to explain myself. I will only be the burden, the pocha, the Malinche, the disgrace. If they are hungry enough to make me understand them, I will wrap their burrito tightly and make the right change for their five-dollar bill. I will fill their cups with extra ice and shout *gracias* with the ring of the cowbell on the door, punctuating hot air. Then I'll slip quietly back behind the swinging doors into a corner of my father's kitchen where no one can see what's on my tongue.

tamal pot

fill the olla with water
fill it with choice cuts
pile fuel bones beneath

in this vessel
you are knit
a vapor fills your lungs
a penny rattles on tin

your masa
and flesh congeal
thick velvet
collected in silken leaf
in corrugated husk
parts melding parts dissolving

maybe it is metal maybe
it is clay
maybe you are smashed between others

a twin brother or a dozen almost
like you almost mirror reflections

feet to the fire you boil on the bottom
tops pop over exposed
evidence of a maker

corporeal kettle
is your bedroom
cast cauldron
your warm evening bath

fire and water and air
space out evenly over your skin
a birthmark
by flame

—*el pensamiento*

Ocean

Ricky and I were swimming in the Pacific Ocean, the cold seaweed broth off the San Diego coast, when we felt a sting.

It was our customary summer family vacation—away from desert heat, away from Tucson, away from the Molino. Ricky was growing taller than me back then, but I was still responsible for him. We bobbed and drifted and I didn't notice we'd floated far from our beach picnic, where our parents and our California cousins ate hot dogs and potato chips, telling jokes by the bonfire.

We were looking only in the direction of the watery horizon, and never looked back. The sun was setting and we were lifted and pulled farther and farther out to sea. I could see Ricky getting smaller but still laughing like salt water. The drifting was like a frothy bubble; we heard nothing and feared nothing in the waves.

Then a faint voice reached us from shore. It was stern and static, repeating a warning. I heard it slowly and understood it slowly. Suddenly I realized I had crossed an invisible barrier in the water I didn't even know existed. We'd gone too far, and the undercurrent was coming.

I motioned to Ricky that we had to swim back; the lifeguard came into view, and his repetitive words grew impatient with how slowly we learned. We paddled ourselves away from the invisible line. We drew closer and closer to shore, and the fear of punishment took over the fear of undercurrent.

When we arrived on the beach, my father yelled at us in front of our cousins. Someone put a towel around me while my father shouted impossible questions—the ones asked by parents who don't really want the answers: *What is wrong with you? What were you thinking?*

I shrank in my bathing suit while Ricky ignored the berating by tossing stones onto the bonfire. Embarrassed, I cried a little and my tears raised only more embarrassment. When he walked away in anger, I silently wished for a different father. Then someone put his hand on my back and said, *He was just worried about you, mija.* I was hugged and there hid my face, wet and sanded, in a warm chest by the water.

sea

my hands
stretch the coast
and my voice reaches over
your head under
your legs sweeping you
buoyant like a bubble
boiling salt pot

my east wind is for you
a seabed
clear
dry land dry land dry
wall of water on the right
and on the left

there is a shore
littered with your ropes
your chains and chariots
child your captors are dead
drowned
but what you wish for
is more egypt

—el pensamiento

Stains

I didn't have many dangerous words with my father in his kitchen, no red-hot tantrums nor fiery screams. But we were in some kind of danger at the Molino, and I knew it. I'd watched my father working over a pot of boiling chile, watched him pour close to the edge enough times to know. A kitchen can erupt. Red chile can flow from some buried source, some dormant volcano no one even knew was there. That is the truth about kitchens; they are hazardous places.

Red hot, orange, and purple. A rainbow of chile seeped into my fingertips daily, swirling into microscopic mountain ranges. This stain was more than a nuisance—it was loud—a feverish onslaught of pigment. I thought some people could live like this, but not me. I kept near soap and water. I scrubbed my hands and plucked bits of food from under my fingernails. I rubbed my skin until it returned to its own color, raw and pumped clean.

Chile stains penetrated the weave of any clothing I wore at the Molino, and at home my stained clothes were flung into corners of my bedroom. They gathered with towels, sheets, and socks, where they softened, tenderized, and marinated deeper and deeper into red chile laundry balls. When there was nothing to watch on TV and no friends to call on the telephone, I plucked these items carefully from the laundry basket. I separated them into categories that made no sense to anyone but me, and sprayed them with stain remover. Then, one batch at a time, they were plunged into hot, soapy water. Tossed and yanked, they submitted to crisp water and suds.

When I walked down school hallways or congregated with friends at pizza parlors and arcades, no one would ever notice I'd been stained. I'd take the necessary steps to not be seen that way, to be clean and unashamed. To not be like the dust kicked up behind ranch trucks on narrow, rocky roads or the sap rolling down the green of an agave flanked by thorns. I'd be safe, I thought. I'd be sure.

apples in the grinder

she held her carving knife
clean from the kitchen
when no one was watching
she was thinking about slicing
through and through

sat with herself in the bedroom mirror
in her head stones spinning hard
like fists twisting wet cotton
crying like babies
fat apples in the grinder

but my voice
reached into the mouth a word
a brother name
playing a video game
down the hall from her

his name was the billows
the sparing waves passing over

I went in for them all you see
between the millstones
into the swollen belly of the molino
I came for them all

—*el pensamiento*

Where could we go?

In 1978, a few months after I was born, *Arizona Daily Star* writer Judy Donovan wrote an article about El Presidio, "the tiny neighborhood where it all began for Tucson."* She wrote, "For the handful of first and second-generation Mexican-Americans still living there, El Presidio ended as a truly Mexican neighborhood in the late 1940s and early 1950s when the 'americanos' began pushing northward across Alameda Street from the downtown district."† That is when the new lawyers came, land speculators too, and cleared old adobe buildings for parking lots. My father remembers the Chinese markets and wagon vendors. He remembers the porch sitting each evening and music playing morning and night. But he also remembers urban renewal, when neighbors and family members were displaced, when homes and businesses were demolished. Urban renewal hit the barrios south of Congress the hardest in the 1960s, but some of that momentum seeped north, past the courthouse and into Barrio Presidio, where the molino continued to work as though time could stand still. As though nothing ever changes.

For her story, Donovan interviewed Presidio neighbors Mr. Mario and Mrs. Stella Cota-Robles, Mrs. Maria Diaz-Pulido, Mrs. Julia Valdez, Ms. Alene Smith, Mr. Patrick Hynes, and my tía, Mrs. Soledad Perez. All interviewees mentioned change or resistance to change or what was destroyed or what was about to be destroyed forever. Donavan wrote, "Soledad Perez remembers when speculators sent their representatives around El Presidio in the mid–1950s trying to buy up property. She and her family (eight

---

* Judy Donovan, "El Presidio . . . Where It All Began," *Tucson's Barrios: A View from Inside*, Arizona Daily Star special report, July 16, 1978, 13, 16.

† Donovan, "El Presidio . . . Where It All Began," 13.

sisters and a brother) have operated El Rapido Tortilla Factory on Washington St., the northern boundary of Tucson's original walled presidio, ever since her father began it."* Tía Soledad had already met with gentrifiers: "She said entrepreneur Lyle Palant offered her $40,000 for her tiny storefront tamale eatery—a tempting amount two decades [earlier]."†

Soledad answered Palant's question with a question: "But where could we go?"

Donovan says that like urban renewal developers before him, "Palant was announcing grandiose plans for the entire vacant block bordered by Church, Council, Court and Meyer. . . . Palant promised to build a $16 million development of offices, apartments, hotel, stores, and a 900-car parking garage there."‡

All this was said before I walked the Presidio streets. All this was happening long before I was born, before Ricky was born. It was fated, perhaps, like writing on the wall—words for a king, a prophecy of numbering, weighing, and then a breach. All this was a story probably much older than we can know, bigger than we can hold in our hands. Donovan must have seen this through some tiny crack in the sidewalk, must have had an inkling of what we used to be and what we could lose. She wrote about what lies beneath the concrete and asphalt on the corner of Washington and Church, the ruins of a prehistoric pit house, the bones that might prove "Tucson is the oldest continuously occupied community in the country."§

---

* Donovan, 13.
† Donovan, 13.
‡ Donovan, 13.
§ Donovan, 16.

Becoming Mr. Rapido

My father grinds himself to the bone in hopes of securing the customers that come to the Molino. I stand by and watch as they step through the front door and peer into the deli case. He shouts a greeting like a prodigal father. He speaks to them as though he

FIGURE 9 Tony Peyron in front of the El Rapido mural in the 1990s. Photo from author's personal collection.

has known them for ages, even if they are new to town. Welcoming them with a smile and a handshake, they sense the building is falling in around them, but my father does everything he can to get them to come again and again. He offers samples. He advertises specials on sidewalk sandwich boards covered in his nearly illegible handwriting. He calls everything *muy, muy bueno*. Over a glass display case presenting napkins, forks, my homemade beaded jewelry for sale, and shame-inducing personal checks stamped with "INSUFFICIENT FUNDS" in red ink, he greets them over and over. He brushes the hair out of his eyes as customers stare at the Pepsi menu board. If it has been a while since their last visit, he yells out, *There he is!* Others look up from the deli case filled with sodas, Snickers, and Twix, acknowledging the customer whom even they might not have seen for a while.

What can I do for you, señor? my father says. He holds the answers in wax paper and Styrofoam.

I never worry about whether or not customers will return to the little tamal factory in the middle of Tucson's growing downtown restaurant arena. This is no concern of mine. But he worries. He wonders if they will forget about him, forget about what he does all day long—for them. It keeps him up some nights. Slowly, they stop coming. Or something else is coming. Fast. Either way, my father in the early morning hours by the molino looks dazed in his apron. The loss of customers is worse than the loss of money—it will eat away at the man he is trying to be, eat away at Mr. Rapido.

Watching him scurry around the garage kitchen, we do not comfort him. We do not seek solutions. My family watches him fall down and get back up, day after day. We don't care if he gets lonely. We go on with our lives, the lives we are creating for ourselves away from the Molino. We are people who ask for work when it is convenient and abandon him when it isn't.

There are few things worse than laboring over food that won't get eaten.

There may be nothing worse than throwing away his food. These are his provisions. This labor is the way we need each other. The way we do family. I won't realize it for many years, but my father's food is a manifestation of service and sacrifice—the very things I've learned love is made of.

I might actually come to understand this. But not everyone understands. Not everyone sees what is so appealing about food cooked in too much lard and salt. It is hard to see it. It is hard to find in a room with no chairs and no tables. When it comes at the hands of someone wearing the same dirty apron for a week, at the face dripping with sweat. When the chile doesn't taste the same as it did yesterday. When the place around the corner is shiny and new. It is hard to see the need for burned offerings, the need for your firstborn.

Because Change Is Not Good

Long before the *Tucson Weekly* newspaper voted El Rapido 1995's Best Mexican Restaurant Without a Dining Room, Tony had a vision. He started dreaming lots of dreams. He was inspired by a photo he saw of my nana's sister, Maria, on her wedding day, cutting the cake in the old house next to the Molino. There were tables with tablecloths, real plates and real flatware all laid out in the zaguan. He imagined a dining room for everyone. A banquet. A party that could happen every day in the old house where so many barrio memories swirled in and out of adobe rooms. In

FIGURE 10 A wedding reception, held in the old house in 1954. *Left to right:* The groom, Frank Spatafore; the bride, Maria Perez; mother of the bride, Martina Perez; two wedding guests; the maid of honor, Josephine T. Salazar; the best man, Ronald J. Perry; and the father of the bride, Aurelio Perez. Photo from author's personal collection.

the end, my tías Soledad, Aurelia, Maria, Angelita, Guadalupe, Micaela, and Aurora, and my uncle Mike, didn't let him transform El Rapido from a lunch counter into a real restaurant. Sometimes people think it was the City of Tucson that prevented dreaming. Or the government. Or some other devil. But it was familia.

My father had already hired Tucson artist Edna Yrigoyen to help him plan the space. I remember the day she came to the Molino and rolled out scrolls of architectural drawings over stainless steel tables. They may have been the biggest sheets of paper I had ever seen. I remember gazing at lines drawn to show how the house could transform into a beautiful dining room. I remember how excited my dad was. But the tías made Tony put away his expensive blueprints and American dreams. Nana kept quiet. Tata stayed out of it. Los Perez had the last say—there would be no El Rapido Mexican *Restaurant*. No shiny ceramic plates and drinking glasses. No seated eating and drinking. No place to stay. No welcoming through front doors into hearths that smelled of oregano and chile.

My father says the family just wanted to keep things the same, didn't want to change or incur expenses. They needed his monthly rent checks, and didn't want to sell the building to him. I never heard the tías or anyone else in the family speak about these dreams and requests; those conversations were kept hidden from me. And I tell myself I know the reasons. I know there should be no tables or menus or waiters floating around in the house where you grew up. When parents and grandparents pass away, we don't feel comfortable with life moving on in what used to be our living room; we don't welcome new bodies inhaling and exhaling in the rooms where ancestors slept, nor in the zaguan where they sang Christmas songs or smoked cigarettes watching lightning storms. A home isn't a public place. It is not a restaurant. A neighborhood isn't a tourist attraction. A presidio must be fortified.

Instead of expanding, there would be contraction. There would be a crushing, corn grinding and counter orders and a kitchen behind swinging doors— a private place like a heart tucked into a chest, a dark interior for my family to keep their imaginations and memories and broken furniture from the light of day. Because change is not good. Not when it reminds you of what you lost.

pooling

a man built a house of his own
on a hill by my barbed crosses
arms stretched out
pleading

concrete and wrought iron
bricks spread on mortar
like masa

a room for sons
on the west side
another for mijitas
facing east
sleeping to the sound
of circling desert bleat

a man dug two holes
one for fire
the other for water
roof diving

no one knows how much this cost
the grinding hours
what amount of tugging at meat equals a pacific
style kidney shape
watering hole

what makes a splash
what prevents drowning

he drained the hole
the clouds rolled in
pooling homes
for sap beetles and redheaded centipedes
toxic toads and snakes
oily and green bottomed

a man swims into
ymca every morning
takes his towel downtown

but the pool
in his own backyard
is harboring grudges

so I press
it close to caliche earth
feed it a deluge
tell it to wait
a little longer
for the sea to swallow it up

—el pensamiento

PART V

Recipe

My father, Tony, is from the west side, and my mother, Anna, the east side. He was born in Arizona, she in California. My mother's parents are from the campos and my father's parents are from the ranchos. My father's favorite color is green, my mother's red. He makes conversation with everyone, but she stays quiet. My father is blind in one eye, and my mother has eyes on the back of her head. My father doesn't wash his hands enough. My mother carries hand sanitizer. My father was born in 1944 and graduated high school a year late, in 1963. My mother was born in 1956 and graduated early, in 1974. My father drinks but doesn't smoke; my mother smokes but doesn't drink. My father speaks one kind of Spanish and doesn't care what people think. My mother speaks another kind of Spanish and cares what everyone thinks. My father's father was in the navy. My mother's father was in the army. He moves fast. She is cautious. He spoils children with junk food. She used to try to feed us tofu.

Combine.

Stir.

Grind.

Let sit in an icebox overnight. Grind again. Repeat.

Sift into a fine, glossy dust, ancestral and translucent. When needed, cure in the sun. Sprinkle on your enchilada casserole, over caldo de queso, or add to your spinach smoothie. Good on a squash blossom quesadilla or shaken in bloody mary mix. Powder over coconut paletas or dredge through with fresh watermelon.

Cover. Let rest.

Desert Dreams

My earliest dream is the desert, Ricky and I walking barefoot on sharp rocks. The dream is crossed with memories, hinging together what really happened and what I must have imagined. In the blur, Ricky is a baby following behind me, his thick legs, creamed skin, and wide feet mimicking mine. He is next to me, a twin set of eyes and fingers and tongue.

Each morning, we feel the urge to walk away from home. We wake from dreams of a desert beckoning us. Ricky can be coaxed from his crib without crying. I help him swing his body over the rails and his toes touch the floor one at a time. I can reach the keyhole to the front door. I know which gold key opens it. Mama is asleep upstairs and can't hear us wiggling out; she sleeps through the sound of a turning knob and wrought iron slamming behind. We step out into the heat or the cold, the sun or the clouds, and immediately make our way away from everything that is secure. Half-dressed in pajamas, or less, we traverse the porch. We exit through an unlatched gate, and creep over shale and limestone. There are thorns of every sort here. Most penetrate for a moment but sting for longer. We toddle between the patches of prickly pear with their long, white taper thorns, barrel cactus with their hooked yellow spines, cholla like Velcro. Outside is limitless. Fences have gates, pathways can be made anywhere, and Ricky and I will survive early-morning walks in the Sonoran Desert again and again. We will walk through imaginary doors and climb through windows that hang from imaginary posts. There are no desert walls in my childhood. I don't know what makes us walk back through our front door, back home as Mama sleeps with the curtains drawn dark in her upstairs bedroom. We make it back unharmed every time. We are admitted over and over, like sunrise.

When I sleep, it looks different. The desert in my dreamworld collapses and fits into a picture frame. It is squares and triangles and intersecting lines, shapes standing in for rocks, cacti, and sunlight. I am in the corner of the picture frame and a shadow grows and grows on the canvas toward me. It bubbles and expands. It presses me hard against the frame. My neck twists and my body cramps as the blob of desert pieces squishes me out of the picture until I awake in panic. Ricky has left me. He should be here, processing through dreams with me, but he has climbed out of his crib on his own. I scale the staircase to Mama's room and Ricky is already there sleeping beside her. I try to tell her why I'm afraid of sharp edges, picture frames, squares and triangles swallowing me, but I don't have those words. *A bad dream*, she explains, and she pulls me into bed with her and Ricky. The dream is gone. I am no longer cowering in the corner of a picture frame, getting smaller and smaller, rolling into a tiny dot, shrunken and invisible. The dream is gone.

The Best Mexican Food?

In her weekly column in the *Tucson Citizen* newspaper, celebrated writer and Tucsonense Alva B. Torres wrote about Tucson food and heritage. In one column, she discussed Tucson as the Mexican Food Capital of the World. Appearing next to advertisements for Hoover vacuums and movie theater screening announcements for *The Mission* and *The Color Purple*, Torres's column effectively listed and described all Tucson's major Mexican food places in a few hundred words. She described their flavors, styles, family lineages, and legacies. She offered some history and statistics. Torres even compared Tucson food with Mexican food from the rest of the Southwest. Near the end of the article she writes, "Mexico has good food, but they should taste a burro from El Rapido."*

---

* Alva B. Torres, "The Best Mexican Food? In Tucson, Of Course . . . ," *Tucson Citizen*, January 20, 1987, 34.

A Name That Means Fire

In third grade, I had an hour of religion class every day, but no one could answer my questions about God. I was embarrassed about my doubt and didn't want other students to hear, so after class one day, I found the courage to ask my teacher, Mrs. King, if I could talk to her. She was a kind woman who managed to make every student feel like a teacher's pet. She wore her hair short and she wasn't a nun. She seemed smarter than other adults. I knew I could trust her. After all the other kids had run out for recess, I told her, *I am not sure if I believe in God.*

Mrs. King acknowledged my words with a look of concern and a gentle hand on my back. She walked me over to the crowded bookcase that stretched out wide below a courtyard window. She knelt down beside me, pulled out a paperback copy of *The Lion, the Witch and the Wardrobe,* and said, *It is OK to doubt. Everyone has doubts.* She put the book in my hands and said it would help.

I glanced at the illustrated drawing of the lion on the cover, the penciled curve and curl of the lion's mane, but I didn't say anything. She insisted I take it home and read it. I stared out the window with disappointment, wondering why Mrs. King wouldn't just tell me the truth. What did this kid's book have to do with anything? It didn't even have the word *God* in the title. I decided not to read it.

My mother's mother, my nana Aurora, died of cancer in the middle of my ninth-grade year. She had been diagnosed with breast cancer, spent five years in remission, then was diagnosed again and died at home on the Tuesday night after my fifteenth birthday. I remember my mother walking into my bedroom the night Nana died to tell me my grandmother was gone, but I sprung up from sleep before she said a word, somehow knowing her news before she spoke it. I remember going into my nana's bedroom to say good-bye, but I couldn't speak. I had been praying for her healing or for her relief, but after Nana died, I started praying to her instead of God. I wrote letters and essays to her. I had lots of words, but they all came after she was gone.

———————

I was in eleventh grade when my mother forced me to make the sacrament of confirmation at Our Mother of Sorrows church.

I'd only be confirming a lie, I said, *I don't believe in any of it*. She already knew that, and I suspected that she might be questioning it all too, but it didn't matter. She insisted.

You just have to, she said.

For a while, I believed that my mother's dead mother had the power to make my mother say these words. Almost everything miraculous or spiritual or Godlike seemed to revolve around Nana Aurora's ghost when I was a teenager. By insisting that I get confirmed, my mother seemed to obey a dead person.

You have to because when I baptized you, I made a promise, my mother said. *You have to do this, and after this, you can do whatever you want.*

She didn't want any blood on her hands. My being confirmed in the Catholic Church meant that she had done everything she could do. She couldn't be held responsible after this. For some reason, this made sense to me, and I relented for my mother's sake. I didn't want my dead grandmother to be disrespected.

Sister Rose, a woman I'd lacked all respect for since I had her as a seventh-grade math teacher, selected me to speak at the confirmation ceremony, which was supposed to be an honor. She required me to write my speech weeks before confirmation, so that she could read a draft before I read it aloud at mass. I did as I was told, and Sister Rose approved of my words.

But the night before confirmation, I was troubled by my drafted speech. I ripped up the pages and threw them away. Then, in a spiral notebook, I wrote a new version of the speech. This one was more honest, at least I thought so, and I felt better. I decided not to show it to Sister Rose.

In the sanctuary of Our Mother of Sorrows church on Tucson's east side, I wore a pale-yellow dress with pink flowers. My friends from school, all kids I figured didn't believe this stuff any more than I did, sat with me in pews in their spring colors. The priest wore Pentecostal red. I shuffled in my seat in anticipation of my speech, but a bigger part of me was self-assured.

When I began my speech, Sister Rose stared at me. Everyone stared. I didn't say anything particularly salacious. There was no sarcasm or shaking of my fist or pounding the podium. But I did make claims. I said, as mildly as I could, that the church was not perfect, that it had never been perfect. This was not an acceptable claim, I knew, and I imagined that simple statement spreading wide, setting the sanctuary ablaze. I let the congregation know what I thought—that we had the responsibility of making this better. I had no intentions of staying in the church, and in my own way, I judged them for staying by telling them that the community needed to do better. This was my way of letting them be OK with sticking to this thing I called a lie. My speech, in my opinion, had very little to do with God.

After reading my confirmation speech, I saw Mrs. McLaughlin, who had been my sixth-grade teacher. In the pews, I noticed her nose and her hands first. She was a tall woman with red hair. Her daughter was in my class, and so Mrs. McLaughlin was often a mother and teacher simultaneously in my eyes. I noticed how she was clapping hard after my speech. I don't remember if she wore a scarf on her head that day to cover the effects of her chemo treatments, but I remember it was the last day I would see her.

After the ceremony, when everyone ate cookies and drank lemonade in the parish hall, Mrs. McLaughlin came to tell me what she thought of my speech.

It was really good, she said. She even asked for a copy.

She was the only one to ever talk to me about what I said, the only one to acknowledge my words. Speaking to her in the parish hall, I was humbled. Looking at her scarf-wrapped head, I remembered my nana Aurora. I remembered cancer. And I wondered if Mrs. McLaughlin had asked the priest for permission to stop medication, the way my mother's mother had a few months before she passed. I wondered if, like my nana Aurora, she might also need permission to die.

―――――――――

A year earlier, I had done something else, I figured, that had been sort of revolutionary.

Between bites of quesadillas stretched thin and transparent like frosted windows, between sips of suicide soda or cinnamon iced tea, nibbles of Kit Kats or Snickers bars, and between the sound of the cowbell, I ate up the pages of a book. I unwrapped dog-eared corners. Stuck on some words, I chewed a line over and over, sometimes ten times, before I noticed that I was stuck. I forced my eyes and tongue forward. My lips moved as I read; I whispered the words on the page.

I remember paragraphs stacked like bricks in the only book I ever opened in the Molino.

I don't remember where the book came from, or how I got a hold of it. I wasn't a reader. Generally, I didn't like books—they were heavier than they looked. Their thickness intimidated me, exhausted me before I could get through the first page. I never saw myself in a book. There were no characters that were me. Sometimes I'd page through books of the saints to find my name, but that was it. Generally, I wouldn't even hold a book, so it was strange for me to have one, especially at work. In the kitchen, there were only newspapers, local magazines, and six-inch-thick copies of the Yellow Pages. My father did not keep books in the kitchen, not even cookbooks. I might have brought in a school textbook once in a while when I had to finish homework, but there were no books for pleasure. There were no books for reading. And I was fine with that. I had decided that what people called *literature* was irrelevant to me. Still, there came a day when I was a teenager, when there seemed to be no customers, when I was idle long enough, sitting on a stool in the corner of the kitchen next to the grinder, finding myself lost in a novel.

I remember stopping to cry for a minute in the seventy-third letter of the novel. There, Celie tells Shug that she doesn't pray to God anymore. She is angry with God and says some things that had crossed my mind before, but not yet my lips. I realized that I felt like Celie. Then came Shug's response: an invitation to think of God as something different than an old white man with a gray beard, to reimagine God rather than reject God. I thought I might be sinning at first, but I imagined God differently in that moment too. I wanted to read the page over and over. I hid my face so that no one in the kitchen would see me sob quietly with relief reading Celie's words: "I never truly notice nothing God make. Not a blade of corn (how it do that?) not the color purple (where it come from?). Not the little wildflowers. Nothing."*

By the time confirmation rolled around, I already knew that my name meant darkness, blackness, an absence of light. But amazingly, I was invited to carefully choose a confirmation name—a new name to give myself, a saint's name traditionally, a name that

---

* Alice Walker, *The Color Purple*, 10th anniversary ed. (New York: Harcourt Brace Jovanovich, 1992), 179.

would inspire. It was one of the only freedoms I enjoyed on my day of confirmation, and unlike the confirmation of my Catholic faith, I took it seriously.

I remember sitting on the stairs to my mother's bedroom for hours, searching through two or three books of saint names. I remember feeling some admiration, affection even, for this kind of book—one that held lists, illustrations, names all alphabetized and organized clearly. I liked the distinction of each saint, their special feast day, their special names, their individual contributions.

I could have chosen Aurora, like my maternal grandmother, a name that means hope, the dawn. I could have chosen Juanita, like my paternal grandmother, a name that meant baptism, the monsoons, a name that Francisco Vázquez de Coronado would have chosen for me.

When I came to it, I read the page of the saint name I chose over and over: San Ignacio. I didn't choose San Ignacio for his noble works, not for his face or hair, not because he was Basque like my great-grandmother and not for his prayers, bravery, or faithfulness, not even for his feast day. I just chose his name. I remember my mother thought it was a strange choice. I remember that no one seemed to like the name and encouraged me to reconsider. But I loved the name I gave myself, a name that means fire.

quake

on the third day
continents lifted and
water found fault

when my body was poured out
earth ground itself again
milling borders asunder
showing you I am the way

in 1887
when railcars pushed
steam pride on my pueblo
clocks stopped
and the church bells rang out in sonora
a song of praise
because bells know
this trepidation
I parted hills on their peaks
I barked at villages
rushed the streets
evaporated lakes I made
fish where there were none
shattered glass and mirrors cracked
boulders both sides for you a revolution
I covered the earth and brought it up again
a holy cross
river running both ways
on your boundary
a watershed taken
with all the watopi in it

then there was a sense of
seasickness
in the desert

you can feel it now
still you you you
can feel me moving
your fathers your grandmothers
tell survival stories
to keep up this shaking
mijita do you know what earthquakes sound like
in spanish
can words be measured like waves
behind dust cloud pillars
the unsettled spinning
is my spark
setting grinding stones ablaze
there will always be
a crushing

but I am ignited creosote bush
helping you keep your distance

sometimes change is good
for you a reminding

you may come as you are
but you may not
come as you please

—*el pensamiento*

In the Soil

In the windswept dust circling our house, raised up in the west Tucson Mountains, lives a microscopic spore. It lies dormant until one crouches down and digs into the dirt, bringing it to surface, then into the wind, making germ airborne, free to infect all creatures that breathe.

I've wondered why, through all our shuffling through desert dirt, Ricky and I, our little bodies surrounded by those thorny trees, inhaled and inhaled but never felt ill, never coughed or fell lethargic. Never grew thin.

Lucky, I guess.

Ambos

Simón was the runt of the litter, and it was obvious Mama wanted to save the weakest when she chose him among the other skinny puppies corralled at the Pima Animal Care Center. We named him Simón Limón. His coat was wiry and light brown and his eyes were dark like mine. He was sweet and scraggily and his adoption was meant to make up for the loss of Chiquita, my little blond Labrador, because my father ran her over backing out of our driveway a few months before. Simón didn't look at all like Chiquita. He was a mutt—not any particular breed, and he was a good dog, spending most of his time outside, wiggling all over when we came home. After we'd had him for a few years, we noticed Simón seemed too tired for being a younger dog. Soon he barely moved when we arrived in the driveway at the end of Molino workdays. My mother took him to the vet and we learned why the dog had been sluggish, and why the flesh on his abdomen became so fine it exposed a clear outline of his ribs, like a rippled terrain. He had valley fever. It was no wonder, since each summer he would burrow into the cool earth just a few inches below the surface of our front-yard wasteland and sleep there for hours. A nose in the dirt was his undoing. In those microbes lay a fungus that struck Simón's lungs, and the vet said we'd have to medicate him for the rest of his life.

When I got a full-ride scholarship to attend the University of Arizona, Mama kept her promise to reward me with a car. She had been promoted to a manager position at AT&T and got a short-term loan to pay for a white convertible Ford Mustang with red interior purchased at a used car lot. It was a car she wished she had had when she was young. My mother wore her nails long and manicured during those years. Her pants and blouses were always ironed with starch and her eyelashes were painted with mascara each morning. Her paycheck far eclipsed my father's, and so the Molino faded in her reality. My new used car was proof of her moving up—like an emblem of American dreams coming true. With the top down all the way from campus up the hill to Paradise Mountain, kicking up dust the whole way, the Mustang finally arrived at our property in the desert to sit in the sun. It was a car that made me change. I started to dress in a different way, and my mother noticed.

When Simón got sick, my mother and father let Ricky and I drive to Nogales in the Mustang to pick up cheap medicine that would keep the dog alive.

―――――――――――

Watching mini dust devils stir up, Ricky and I are headed south on I–19. We pass pecan groves, RV resorts, and sandy washes on our way to Ambos Nogales. Ricky is wearing an L.A. Dodgers baseball cap and my brown, stringy hair is tangling in the wind. I drive fast and the warm air pulls at our skin. As we inch across the ribbed landscape, the border draws us out like an undertow.

When we arrive in Nogales, Arizona, I park the car at McDonald's, like my father taught me to. Ricky and I massage the money in our pockets and walk to the U.S. Customs and Border Protection crossing. It is a concrete hub, and lines of people, fences, or cars spoke out in every direction like a turnstile that only spins one way.

When we make it to the other side, everything is different. Ricky and I walk into Nogales, Sonora, and navigate sidewalks and side streets in a maze of familiar ground. We pass several pharmacies, hoping to extend our errand, and come to a restaurant that we recognize, or think we recognize. We climb a staircase to the dining room built into the rock of a mountainside and find we are the day's first customers. We are seated and served free margaritas that make us talk about things we don't usually talk about.

Ricky stares at the glossy menu. *How did they ever get married?* he asks.

I know he means this more as a comment than a question. *They don't have anything in common,* I say.

I know, he agrees.

It's like they wanted to make things hard on themselves. I actually believe this and imagine a sin that they might be trying to make up for.

The waiter stares at us from the other side of the dining room. I put the menu down. *Do you want to share the fajita plate?*

No, I want my own plate, he says as he watches the waiter pick up his pen and pad.

Contemplating the botanas and main dishes, I wonder when was the last time my mother had been to the Molino. It felt like years. There are only a couple of blocks between her building and my father's in downtown Tucson, but I see that divide growing like a fault line.

My mouth waters a bit and I finally say, *I wonder if Dad has ever said anything nice to her.*

What about Mom? She's the one who dogs him all the time.

I put down the menu again. *Well, so do you.*

Yeah. We all do. It's too easy.

That's true.

True dat.

Shut up.

You shut up.

Should we get an appetizer?

Yeah, a cheesy one.

No, I want guacamole.

You get your own then.

I can't eat a whole appetizer, I say.

Oh yes you can, he says.

Once the food comes, we talk less and eat more, taking this opportunity to use our bodies as dumping grounds for everything we can't seem to figure out or say out loud. Filled and buzzed, we walk back down the streets of Nogales, Sonora. I start to covet all the shiny things in shops, and wish I had money for more than dog medicine. The sidewalks and storefront windows are lined with sunglasses, flower vases, and punched tin mirrors. Leather jackets, silver earrings, and velvet paintings all make me feel like I'm at home. But we are not home. And I begin to realize that bringing these curios home, to my bedroom, would be like a lie. I start to know they aren't real. For a moment, I want to collect these lies. I wade in the water of souvenir shops and feel myself melting into storefronts, their veneers, those layers of blue and green and red. I want to live there for a while, in the rule breaking and mirror reflections of México. I want to stay and I want Ricky to stay too.

When we arrive at our destination, I struggle to explain the drug we need to the pharmacist. *Mi perro. Medicina. Valley fever. Por favor.* The words are wrong because they don't come from me. I don't know how to talk about fungal infections in Spanish. I don't know how to move my lips after this many margaritas. I think, *This is what gringos do in México.* I want my face to say, *I'm not one of them.* In my faltering, I want to say, *Con permiso, my Spanish doesn't live in my mouth.*

Though I have wished for it along the thrashed streets of Nogales, Ricky and I don't grow as transparent as we hoped to be. We teeter on security. On self-doubting. We go back and forth, related, then strangers. We need what this side of the line provides, and yet we can't find the words to ask for what we need. Our words get turned around and then lost on this side. Our words are fenced in with painted faces of coyotes and horses, lizards and sunsets. As the tequila filters itself into our blood, Mexico becomes flowers and stars climbing every shop wall.

We are kids, and not like those who peddle wooden mario-
nettes. When we leave the pharmacy, medicine finally in tow,
we slide back into reality. We are convertible-Mustang-driving,
baseball-cap-wearing, drunk-ass, dog-medicine-buying foreigners.
We are the runts of the litter. We are infected by something, from
the air we breathe, the air on the other side.

As we drive north, I think about the tourist shops displaying
the hundreds, maybe even thousands, of statues of that idol we
have come to discount or protest day after day at the Molino—it
is the Sleepy Mexican, and he is still hiding his face from us.

proof of marriage

your mother is eating dinner
with nick at nite
your father is on family vacations
with other families
and you know why

or think you do
so you remind yourself of pictures
you comfort yourself with
her frosted hair his
face red from sun labor

in crushed velvet photo albums
or in newspaper announcements
you look to men in ruffled collar tuxedos
look to her hand me down patina gown
searching for some proof
you are wondering and wishing
you are looking and not seeing

did mister garcia of la suprema not feed
three hundred twenty-five
barbacoa beans and potato salad
were there no red fondant hearts on a five
tier cake two
days before valentines did
flowers not arrive on time
and mariachi los changuitos feos
not play trumpets and horns
did throats not shout of love for five
paid hours as my people poured into
the hall of remembering

jim beam jose
cuervo cheap champagne bled where red
velvet bridesmaids carried lazos and ramos
and arras and guests from places
smelling like corn came to rest
in the aztec inn or on the maid of honors
couch all to pin dollar bills to white poof
all to affirm two shall become one
telling and retelling love again
more than signatures on paper
mijita

were you not born
new years eve the same year they wed
and is this not enough proof for you
have you not read what I
said I am
not about your breaching

mijita
you already know
hearts harden

but remember I
invented the blood
beating inside them

—*el pensamiento*

Mountain Bells

Mama was at work, on the telephone. Crowned in her Western Electric 52 Bell System Headset, she was talking to someone all day long, dialing numbers, tip testing wires, and pushing cards into her calculagraphs. She was listening carefully for static, the sound that meant she was the only one on a line. She and the other operators sat in a packed room up on the second floor of a modern building on the corner of Alameda Street and Scott Avenue, a block east of all the bones exhaling beneath the Presidio.

Her building still stands, stacked in blue and green brick, shiny smooth and speckled granite with wraparound archways that echo another time and place. There are twelve calls going at once on Mama's board. Blinking lights and bubbles on IBM cards—Mama slashing through marks of numbers needed to dial. Mama remembers the date of her first day at work answering these phones: September 9, 1974. She was days away from her eighteenth birthday. *This is a good job*, her mother assured her. *The utilities companies never go out of business*, she said. Mama kept her Mountain Bell job after she married, after I was born, and after Ricky came, because restaurants come and go but *utilities are secure.*

Just not secure enough. Closing day came. And I remember the rumble in our house. I remember the questions and the anxiety that bills couldn't be covered with the money earned from tamales and tortillas alone.

Mama and the other operators were given the option of being laid off or moving out of state to keep their jobs.

I have to go to Colorado, Mama said.

Well, I'm not leaving the Molino, my father said.

And that was that. The Molino was set in its spot. There was no moving it.

Ricky drove Mama to Denver and she stayed away for a long time. She wore her nails long and bare then. She spent lots of time on the telephone. Not with me, but for me. For all of us.

I didn't want to live in our house on the hill with my father anymore, so I left home after Mama left. I still saw my father each day at the Molino. I saw him grind, then he would go home to an empty house in the desert. We talked, but not about ourselves. Not about how Mama left, how I left, nor about how Ricky was getting ready to leave too. I got a paycheck each week. We didn't talk about the things I was learning at university or the places I wanted to go, the way I wanted to dance or the parts of my heart that had been broken. Mama never came up in conversation over beef we shredded, over eggs we scrambled, or beans we smashed. I never mentioned Mama over the mountains of cheese I piled up on plates. Sometimes my father would make conversation and almost accidentally ask, *Have you talked to your mother lately?*

My answers were one word and no more, like a single bubble slashed through on a punch card.

Mama and I talked on the phone on Sundays, and we had nothing to talk about. We had nothing to listen to, except we were sure to say *I love you* before we hung up. Through the buried conduits of telephone lines, the underground cables like crypts and woven wires like braided hair, we made the best of things. And that was that.

In school, my professors wanted to teach me how to communicate better, but they did not teach me how to talk to my parents. They didn't speak their language. So I never called my mother knowing what to say. I called because not calling would be like being lost.

Before Mama left Tucson, I visited her one last time at the Mountain Bell building. Even though I was already halfway through my credits at the university, I took the operator exam to see if I could go to work at the telephone company, like Mama. I walked from the Molino to her building, and a security guard called her down to escort me in. We took the elevator up and she led me through a switch room that took up an entire downtown Tucson city block. She led me through the aisles of communication computers and conduits, their rainbow cables shooting out and curving over every machine. A mountain of wires tangled there, filling the enormous room from wall to wall and floor to ceiling. I had never seen anything like it.

What is this place? I asked.

Mama answered, *This is how we talk.*

4:00 A.M.

My father wakes early and alone in his house on the hill. He puts on his best socks and most comfortable tennis shoes. He packs water bottles, binoculars, and a blanket into his athletic bag. He remembers to grab his walking stick from the patio. He climbs into his truck and drives to the San Xavier Mission, where he will meet the others. They will caravan or bus together south toward the border. They will pray. They will walk. They will cross.

Making a Manda

It is eighty-seven kilometers from Nogales to Magdalena de Kino. Pilgrims on their manda walk this distance in two days to arrive at the mission church, Santa Maria de Magdalena, to honor San Francisco Xavier. They do it in October, when the weather is fair, on the feast day of another saint with a similar name, San Francisco de Assisi.

These twin names melt together on pilgrimage, one the saint of missions, the other the saint of the natural world. They curl up like the spines of an eagle claw cactus and you can't tell one barb from the other. Spanish baroque churches raise up in the desert. Their dome-top crosses cut through mountain skies. The dirt lifts. They behold each other.

My father begins his pilgrimage on the other side. He walks well. He has always been a good walker, traversing mountains and washes on a hundred different hunting and scouting trips. He can keep going when others must stop. He can last. Even when blisters rise and burst, when the rain pours, when water bottles are empty. My father passes cardboard-patched cinder block houses with corrugated tin roofs. He passes taco trucks and stray dogs, and gas stations fortified with tamaleros.

When my father doesn't walk the full distance of the pilgrimage, he makes another kind of manda: he makes food for the pilgrims. He hands out oranges and water cups. He follows behind the walkers in a slow caravan of trucks. At a ranch near Imuris, the halfway point on his manda, he makes spaghetti for an army of pilgrims, served with bread and beer. He rolls out a sleeping bag with the others and sleeps hard on the bare desert floor.

There is a statue among the pilgrims. There are many statues.

At the beginning, in the middle, at the end of the pilgrimage. They are images of holy men. They are figures carved or molded, painted and patinated. The pilgrims touch those figures cocooned in white robes, feet and hands crossed, lit by moonlight through stained glass, frozen in the desert. Pilgrims reflect and pilgrims cry. They pin ornaments and handwritten letters to the statues. These sculptures are worn and dark and revered as healers when the pilgrims pray desperately to whoever or whatever is in front of them.

Padre Kino's bones are there too, at the end of the pilgrimage. This is where Kino succumbed to fever and was buried or hidden underneath the floor of the chapel of San Francisco Xavier at the Temple of Santa Maria de Magdalena. My father says that no matter what pain he feels on his manda, his feet *do . . . not . . . hurt . . .* when he walks into the mausoleum that holds Kino's crypt.

I wonder if he stops there, if the carved images are the point of this manda, the end that means he turns back to Tucson to return to his empty house with a backyard pool filled with nothing. Or maybe these carved images are pointing to another destination. Maybe. If he keeps going, if he keeps walking, maybe the next figure on the road will be flesh and blood instead.

In the Canyon

I don't understand the point of hiking, Ricky says when he tells us the story of the first time he went on what he called *a real hike.* He explains, *You know, because I'm fat. I don't hike, not on a real hike. But I was told it was going to be easy—a couple of miles and mostly flat.*

He went to Sycamore Canyon in the Pajarita Wilderness with his best friend from school, Al. On a cool morning in October, they traveled south on I–19 and exited on a two-lane highway toward Ruby, Arizona, near the ranch where my father's father was born and raised. From the highway exit, they drove Al's old Jeep about twelve miles southwest to the entrance of the trailhead. They planned to hike all the way into the canyon to where the trail ended at the U.S.-Mexico border.

We had stopped and got Carl's Jr. breakfast sandwiches first, he says. *I remember it was a Saturday and I remember I was wearing cargo shorts and a T-shirt. I had a few twenty-ounce bottles of water with me. And it was perfect weather—like seventy degrees.* Al promised Ricky it would be a perfect day for a beautiful walk in the wilderness.

The trail was almost all shade, and the canyon walls reached twenty feet or more above their heads, like curtains of rock concealing the blue of the sky. *There was this cool spot where the canyon drops in, and there is a pool, maybe twenty by twenty feet around, all rock basin, like a bowl made of rock.* My brother remembers marveling at the pool, he remembers how stumbling upon a body of water in the desert, even in a canyon, is like coming upon a miracle or magic or something so spectacular, you have to stare at it for a long time. *But that pool was too cold and there was so much algae, so I wasn't going in,* he says.

They came to a rocky passage where the canyon crevice comes to a narrow slot with steep sides, and there was a rope hung from above to help guide hikers through the uneven cleft.

They hiked about a mile past the rope before my brother sat on a rock and said, *I'm done.* Al encouraged him, said they didn't have to go all the way to the border and that the main trail ended a few hundred feet away, but Ricky found a soft sandy area he liked. *It was fully shaded. I was so tired and just wanted to take a nap there. It was so nice and I just wanted to sleep. I told him to go ahead on his own and I'd wait for him.* Ricky finished a bottle of water there and closed his eyes in the cool of the afternoon. *Al was right. It was beautiful. It was perfect there.* Ricky slept peacefully for an hour and a half or more in the sand. He finally woke and realized Al still wasn't back. He wondered, *What the hell is taking him so long?*

They had been separated before, but they had remained friends. Once, while very drunk near some nightclub beach party in Puerto Peñasco, México, they lost each other and my brother wandered borracho through the streets until he ended up getting arrested. The officers took everything out of his wallet before putting him in a jail cell filled with other U.S. boys. One boy told him that he had hidden two twenty-dollar bills in his sock. My brother, who is very good at talking, convinced the boy to give him half the cash so they could buy their way out of jail. It worked and Ricky was saved. Shocked but free, he wandered into dawn searching the beach town looking for Al. In a population over fifty thousand people plus spring breakers, my brother and his friend somehow bumped into each other. Penniless and still on edge, they drove home, telling and retelling their frightening and miraculous stories. Once they crossed the border north, they knew they were home free.

Ricky says that back in the canyon, *it was at least 2:30 p.m.* when he awoke from his dry creek bed nap, but in the shadow of the west side of the canyon mountain, it seemed much later. *I was thinking, it took us three hours to get in, it is gonna take about the same to get out.*

The sun goes down about 6:00 p.m., I thought, so I needed to find him or hike out right away to get back to the Jeep before dark.

Ricky first hiked into the canyon a little farther to see what was left of the trail. When he realized it was a few hundred yards more of walkable path, he yelled Al's name as loud as he could, but there was no response. *I wondered if he had passed the walkable trail into the bush toward the border. I wasn't gonna do that,* Ricky says. *Anyway, Al was faster than me. He was in good shape. I figured he'd catch up with me on my way back.* Ricky continued yelling for him on the way back, discouraged by the fact that Al had always had bad hearing and that no one else seemed to be in the canyon with him—no other hikers, no one responding to any of his calls.

I finally got back to the spot with the rope, he says. In the narrow corridor, the mountain sides met face to face, and Ricky passed back through. This is where he realized the trail wasn't so much a trail as it was the water-carved passage at the bottom of the canyon. On the way in, they knew to walk south, but the way out was different.

What you don't realize on the way in is how many smaller waterways funnel into the canyon. Smaller canyons converge. On your way back out, you realize there are other options, forks that you didn't see on the way in. I never noticed. You don't realize when you aren't paying attention. On the way out, the wilderness all looks the same, he explained. It hides an intricate maze. *I mean, I take pride in having a really good sense of direction, and I was like, oh shit.*

When he couldn't tell which way to go and couldn't figure out which way was wrong, Ricky went the directions that felt right to him and he didn't turn back to figure out if he had made any wrong choices. He kept climbing and walking into the branching courses in the canyon and into the dark.

Relieved, he came to the rock basin pool he had seen on the way in. He knew he must be close to the end. Then he saw the Jeep right in front of him. *My heart sank,* he says, *because I had found it completely by accident. It was so dark, I just literally walked into it. I*

couldn't believe it. I was like, thank God, I made it. But his relief was
followed immediately with concern for how Al would find his way
out in the pitch black of the canyon now. *I almost tripped over the
Jeep, so how hard was it going to be for him to find his way?*

Al had the keys to the locked Jeep, so Ricky pushed down one
of the broken windows and climbed in. He turned on the lights
and honked repeatedly to signal Al. *I had hoped he was only about an
hour behind me. I yelled every once in a while,* he says. But there was
nothing else he could do. There were no places close by to walk
to and he didn't have a flashlight anyway. There were no homes,
no ranches. It was a hunting area. Like the nearby wilderness that
my father and grandfather had taken Ricky to so many times in
his youth, this was a desert without safety nets, and Ricky knew it.

*It was after 8:00 p.m. when I got really worried. I started thinking the
worst. Worrying, you know how your mind goes. What if he got hurt?
My mind started making up this crazy shit. I thought, What am I going
to tell his parents? Was this my fault? Should I have gone out there to
look for him? What if he made it back but I got lost instead? The stars
and the moon definitely betrayed me that night.*

Then it started to get very cold. Ricky rolled up the window,
trying to stay warm. There was a T-shirt in the back seat and he
wrapped it around his bare legs. He pulled his T-shirt collar up
around his nose so that he could feel his breath warm on his skin,
but it moistened his shirt, making it wet and icy. He imagined how
much colder it must be for Al out there. He wondered, *How in the
hell are we going to get through this?* He decided to try to sleep, and
when the sun came out, he'd walk out toward the highway. Sleep
didn't come, so he sang some songs to pass the time. To keep
himself together.

Sometimes when my brother tells this story, he says he prayed.
Sometimes he refuses to admit he prayed. I don't know exactly
what may have been whispered in the Jeep that night, the sounds
that took him across the unbearably slow hours bringing up a
Sunday morning.

When the sun rose and Al had still not returned, Ricky figured he was in serious danger and probably hurt. *I knew we needed search and rescue. I drank another bottle of water, saved one bottle in the Jeep for Al, and saved one for my walk out. I got out of the Jeep and realized it hadn't been any warmer inside than it was outside. I couldn't believe it.* In the freezing cold, Ricky started walking back to I–19 alone.

More than an hour into his walk toward the highway, he spotted a car coming his way. It was three hikers driving to the same canyon trail Ricky had walked out of. *They were three old men. I flagged them down and explained everything. Two were cool, wanting to help, but the third, the driver, he seemed bothered. It was weird. He seemed annoyed by me, like I was this dumb, unprepared kid ruining his perfect day for a beautiful hike.* But Ricky is a good talker. He convinced them to drive him back away from the canyon to find help.

They drove for about fifteen minutes before they found a Border Patrol agent parked on the side of the road. Satisfied, the three old men left Ricky with the Border Patrol agent and drove away.

I told him the whole story and the agent just said, "Yeah, OK," like it was no big deal. The agent wasn't alarmed or even surprised. He wasn't in a hurry either, and this made my brother even more distressed. Ricky imagined Al had little time to spare if he was really hurt, and so he got very frustrated when the agent wanted to drive all the way back to the Jeep before calling for help. *I finally just said, FINE. I figured he probably had to radio in the exact coordinates and he promised that when they got back to the Jeep, he would call for a helicopter.* So the Border Patrol truck took my brother back south toward the border, back into the canyon.

It had been almost two hours since Ricky had set out walking that morning when they approached where the Jeep was parked, and there they found Al standing in his underwear.

Ricky's relief was immediately followed by shame and bewilderment. He worried the agent wouldn't believe his desperate story. He imagined the agent thinking something "funny" was going on, and this embarrassed him. In his best Texas accent,

Ricky imagined the agent asking himself, *What kind a hiking you boys doing out here?*

Ugh. I couldn't believe it, Ricky says. *I saw him and I was like, what the hell?*

There was some *Dude, are you OK?* questioning, back and forth, before the stories came out fast and agitated. Al explained that he had gotten lost. When it got dark, he found a cavernous spot and laid down, covered himself with leaves to keep warm, and slept there, alone in the canyon. At first light, he made his way out. He ran out of drinking water, so when he got to the canyon's pool he reached down to retrieve a bottle full, but slipped on the algae and fell into the icy water. Completely soaked, he had to take his wet clothes off to keep from freezing to death.

Telling and retelling the details of what they had experienced, Ricky and Al watched each other's breath evaporate into the cold canyon air. As the Border Patrol agent drove away, they allowed themselves to imagine all the things that didn't happen, all the things they were spared. They climbed back into the Jeep and drove back to Tucson. In the end, they found they were not mad at each other for being so very lost.

rope

mijitos y mijitas
this is the soundtrack for real

it is a blockbuster I've been screening
since time a projection
on this wall with you

watch me
draw a word in the silt
draw your name in the rain clouds

gold hunting
grandfathers
make many patrols and peace
treaties in the desert
wilderness

but I keep promises beyond
forty year covenants

did you see my pool
did you go down to the wash
did it make you well

on a long stretched out sandy sunday
the earth shades and shakes
the grinding whips out boys and their broken windows

my glory passes you by in a canyon cleft

mijo
my rope is for you

—*el pensamiento*

Eulogy

The heaviest man I ever met was a friend of my father's who worked at the Molino, wheeling around an oxygen cart tethered to his nostrils. His breathing machine bumped and rolled around the kitchen, awkward around corners and squeezing into small spaces where it didn't belong. Even with assistance, he struggled to breathe. The man's thinning and greasy black hair matched the shine on his black-rimmed glasses. His mustache was wide above his mouth, and his bloated fingers wrapped tight around the post of the oxygen cart as he maneuvered from one position to the next. He was a short man, exactly my height, and his underbelly was often fully exposed under a tight white cotton T-shirt.

My father met his sick friend in the Army National Guard when they were both in their early twenties. They both worked kitchen patrol, serving up enormous quantities of food in five-gallon drums stacked from floor to ceiling. My father remembers that he couldn't do much with that food—there were no spices to flavor the meals and no ingredients to change the dietary supply from matching the same color of pots and pans or uniforms and lace-up boots. I understood that army food was thick, peeling, and scabrous. It was as tiresome as orders shouted out eight hours a day, but it was enough to survive, and was even enjoyed by some soldiers.

His grandfather Aurelio had taught him sabór, but cooking the army way taught my father how to make breakfast, lunch, and dinner for the masses—how to make do for a village of the hungry. It gave him a new way to live a kind of scullery brotherhood, a way to make a friend who was a trusted laborer and ally in the kitchen.

My father's sick friend worked sporadically at El Rapido. Every few years, he'd show up, seemingly bigger than before, and my father never turned him away. Toward the end of his life, he could barely stand or walk, so my father usually sat him in the corner of the kitchen to clean elotes, to remove the green husks from each ear of corn one by one. His belly covered his legs all the way to his knees when he sat, so he couldn't pile the fresh corn husks from elotes on his lap like everyone else. Instead, he stacked them in tall green piles on a side table that my father would position next to him. On the other side, my father would take a machete to each ear and throw them in a bin beside his friend, crowding him into heaps of corn for hours.

I did my best to avoid those crowded spaces.

I can't remember if it happened by accident or if I consciously chose to, but I was not kind to my father's friend. I didn't take the opportunity to learn anything from him other than how to be ashamed of so much exposed flesh and wheezing in the kitchen. He was polite. He was even kind to me, but I wanted to be the opposite of him, so I often refused to engage or even respond when he talked to me. I hated that he shared a name with my brother. I hated that when he stood in front of me, we could see eye to eye. I never said it out loud, but I was terrified of becoming him. Looking at his body made me hate mine even more, made me feel a weight I didn't want to feel, a gross harness of fat that pulled me under. I didn't want this in my family.

My father's friend was slowly dying, but I don't remember having or showing any sympathy for his condition. My only thought was *The kitchen is not a place for dying.*

I wasn't at work in the Molino the day my father's friend passed away. When my father got home, he set his briefcase down, sat at the kitchen counter, and called me. With a remnant of shock, he told me the news. The first thing I imagined was an accident. I feared a fall or a sharp object or a fire. I don't know why exactly, but I thought something horrible and gruesome must have happened.

He said he had to go to the bathroom, you know, and I didn't think anything, my father began to explain. *He walked out the door and into the old house and I didn't see anything wrong. I was busy, you know. I had a big order. Then I realized he had been gone too long. I was getting worried 'cause he was taking too damn long in the bathroom, you know what I mean?* My father shook his head. *So I went to check on him. I called his name a hundred times, but he didn't answer. I called and called, but nothing. So I opened the bathroom door and he was in there. I yelled at him, but he wasn't moving. Man, I didn't know what to do. I didn't know what happened. I just ran into the Molino and called 911.*

And they came, you know, but it was too late I think. He wasn't responding, you know what I mean? There was nothing I could do.

My father is not the type of person to cry. He didn't shed any tears in front of me over his friend or a few others who passed over the years, ill or not, dying before their time. His words that day were the only eulogy I ever heard, the only thing resembling an altar, a retablo, a candle and flowers—our only picture of this man's heavy, resting glory.

the day and the hour

not even
the angels in heaven
know when the flood is coming
when the thief is at the door

two sisters
will be grinding
one will be taken
and the other left

—*el pensamiento*

Closing

I'll tell you what they say happened.

My father says it was the payroll taxes that broke the camel's back. Sometime before Thanksgiving of 2000, he says his long-time accountant, Mr. Richard Meyers, gave him the bad news. El Rapido owed $4,200 in taxes that had to be paid by December 31. It was more money than any of us had. My father told me the story of how Richard Meyers went down to talk to the feds with him, to request a provision. He asked, *Can we make payments to keep the Molino alive?* But their request was denied.

My father says it was some kind of revision in the tax law; he says that other businesses were hit hard too that same year. He mentioned a Mr. Quintero who had to close his painting business, then there was a hardware store and a Chinese market forced to close too, he claimed. They say Montgomery Ward's two Tucson locations were also closing, leaving two hundred souls out of work.[*]

My father complained of other problems. There were rising fees for wastewater service and garbage collection. There were serious building repairs needed that no one could pay for. There were increased costs for supplies. And of course, there were all the changes in the city—a mass exodus of small business owners because no one would come downtown anymore. Dozens of downtown shops closed in the late 1990s; they were listed in the newspaper with discussions of what was happening to the heart of the city—that it was missing a few beats, maybe. That it was in

---

[*] "Businesses Close," *Tucson Citizen*, January 2, 2001, 8.

decline. Some said a new era was coming, and not everyone who was there was supposed to be anymore.

My nana Juanita joined in the voices telling the same tale. She said business was down. *One day he only had one customer*, she said. I imagined this a gross exaggeration, but I know it is possible. Either way, my father was *very disappointed*, she said.[†] Her son was working sixty-five to seventy-five hours a week, but it wasn't enough. It was never enough.

———

I'll tell you what didn't happen.

———

My father didn't get a loan to pay for the taxes. He didn't accept help from anyone who'd talked to the city council and the office of economic development on his behalf.[‡] My father didn't ask the tías for help either. He never had a going-out-of-business sale or a closing party. There were no songs sung and no flags raised. There was no wake and there was no funeral.

———

I'll tell you what did happen.

———

On December 24, 2000, the Molino shut its doors for the last time. My father asked me to write a note for customers, letting them know that it was over, so I wrote the message in blue ink on a

---

[†] "Tucson Industry: Retail," *Arizona Daily Star*, December 29, 2000, 37.

[‡] Oscar Abeyta, "High Costs Bring El Rapido to Stop after 67 Years," *Tucson Citizen*, December 27, 2000, 10.

sheet of wax paper from the kitchen. It was about two sentences long, but I don't remember what the exact words were. No one does. I hung it in the window with tape and it remained there, side by side with the Sleepy Mexican, for weeks or maybe months. That's how the news spread, without detail, to our city.

My father asked me to write a letter too, addressed to the tías and Uncle Mike, the inheritors of the property at the northeast corner of Washington and Meyer to whom he had been paying monthly rent for the business. My father's youngest sister, Yvette, had suggested it—she said that there needed to be better communication between the family and that my father could offer an apology in a letter. I wrote it, but I don't think it did any good. I tried to make my words my father's words, so I didn't really apologize. As far as I know, there was never a response. I'm not even sure if my father ever sent the letter.

I was told that after the Molino closed, my nana Juanita was removed by her siblings from all documents naming her in any part an inheritor of her father's Presidio property. But that could be a fabrication too. It could be that she was never going to inherit anything after she got married and after her brother was finally born.

Things were never the same after that. Everyone has reminded me of how close my father's family was. How they were inseparable. With the Molino's closing, a deep-seated resentment or miscommunication or both between my father and his family began to replace whatever had been there before.

———

I'll tell you what I tell myself.

———

On December 24, two thousand years after the birth of our Lord, the Molino, age sixty-seven, passed away quietly in its home on the corner of North Meyer and West Washington in Tucson, Arizona. Though the exact date of birth is unknown, the Molino grew up in an adobe structure used as both business and residence, as was the custom in Barrio Presidio. The Molino was employed for all its years as both market and lunch counter, serving tortillas, tamales, quesadillas, burritos, and tacos. Opened and operated by Aurelio and Martina Perez, the Molino passed to the Perezes' eldest daughter, Soledad, and was finally attended by its last and faithful servant and the Perezes' grandson, Mr. Tony Perez Peyron. The Molino employed four generations of the Perez and Peyron family. Exact numbers are not recorded, but family estimates suggest that several dozen Tucson souls lived and/or worked at the Molino. Notable visitors include Raúl Castro, the first Mexican American to be elected governor of Arizona, golf pro Nancy Lopez, and there was that one time . . . when former president Bill Clinton's limousine drove by our Sleepy Mexican but decided to give patronage to the famed El Charro Café located around the corner from the Molino at 311 North Court Avenue.

The Molino's death came suddenly, at least to most family and community members. Casa Herrera, molino manufacturer of Los Angeles, had provided the last grinding stones to be used in the Molino, which my father had recently purchased from Mr. Herrera for $300. Though the grinder had suffered some illness in the decades prior to death, including a possible threat from urban renewal enthusiasts in the 1960s, it was in full throttle during the Christmas tamal season the year it closed. This resilience is what many will remember fondly. The Molino provided survival for many souls. Its grinding made many things possible. The process was not lost for all. Sadly, in its last days, the Molino's value has been obscured, ravaged by at least two generations of language attrition, ethnic rejection, gentrification, cultural appropriation, and assimilation.

Funeral services will not be held at the San Augustín Cathedral, 192 South Stone Avenue, nor shall there be any rosary recitation with a morning Mass. No interment will follow at Holy Hope Cemetery. The family has declined any requests for visitation. No arrangements will be made by CARRILLO'S TUCSON MORTU-ARY. In lieu of flowers and cards, the family has requested privacy.

Familial dissolution will usher in the erasure of the Molino's memory from the Presidio's conscience. Unsolicited visitations may not be welcomed, but viewing of the Molino's decades-old mural of the Sleepy Mexican is open to the public— an ideal option for well-wishers, pilgrims, pillagers, photographers, illustrators, sightseers, sin vergüenzas, malcriados, opportunists, and those who mourn. Blessed are those who mourn.

PART VI

Whispering Wall

I was not a believer. I regarded Jesus as a stone figure, a statue, often bloodied and weeping. He appeared regularly in my life. Like the Sleepy Mexican, he was always there. Jesus was on funeral cards and tall candles lit in churches I frequented, on velvet paintings hung in dining rooms, set in ink on every shade of skin, in front-yard altars and backyard gardens, in ceramic figures grazing the ceilings over grocery store shelving, and on thick blankets hanging from clothing lines at the swap meet. He was the shape of gold pendants and silver belt buckles, the size of rosary beads and miniature cloth scapulars. He was made of everything but flesh, and so I never saw his heart beating.

I thought of him as a fictional character in a book. I thought everyone did. But my family taught me that there are places in stories where words are made flesh. There are times when thoughts incarnate. On the border, there are places like miracles, like little balls of dough electrified. I heard a still, small voice underneath the hum of the molino; I remembered a sound like distant thunder. I heard a person speaking to me. So I tried speaking back.

Nixtamalization

Corn is too coarse. It is abrasive. Unrefined. Its thick skin is too raw for the molino, not ready to be pushed between stones, so there is a boiling, a chemical agent, a wood ash to denature it, to break protein into surrendering seed.

There are different ways to split open.

Like an alkali, there are many englishes, many colonizers, and many conquerors. They are a slaked lime or slurry. They are the whitewashing I think I can escape or the sugar-powdered pop-overs I refuse to let be tossed in the trash, a calcium hydroxide bath making me clean, altering me and my heart, making me ready for grinding.

Like all of creation, corn will genuflect.

They say change is not good. They say change is good.

My father says, *Hey, let me tell you something, OK? Everything changes.*

Jackpot

Everyone was worried about what would happen to Tony Peyron, but I left Tucson a few weeks after the Molino closed anyway. I was finally out of the kitchen and everything was green. I left the Sonoran Desert and went where there was water all year long. There was always water. For a few hours every day, I danced. I stared at my body in mirrors and made all my parts move. I wore short skirts and low-cut tops and didn't apologize for it. I started to read books. I fell in love. I spent lots of time looking out the window at cottonwood trees. Sometimes I swept my kitchen floor and sometimes I went home to visit Nana and Tata in Barrio Menlo.

I didn't see much of Tony Peyron because he was usually at work. He found a job cooking tamales and hamburgers and french fries at an offtrack betting bar. He found his forty hours a week like everyone else. But the cigarette smoke bothered him, so he applied to work in a casino café on the Tohono O'odham reservation instead. There he was surrounded by Mexicans cooking and Indians managing and lots of people looking for their fortunes. After my mother, my brother, and I had all left him alone in his house on a mountain, Tony Peyron made more money per hour than he had ever made in his life. Sleeping alone in his crumbling house on a hill, my father finally started earning a retirement. He still told stories lit by a fierce kitchen fire every morning. And everyone still raved about his food. *Man, I hit the jackpot*, he said. But everyone knows a job isn't enough.

On Wednesdays and Saturdays, he'd sit down at his kitchen counter and on scraps of paper he'd pen the numbers he would play that week. Sometimes a trifecta for the dog races, sometimes a series of six numbers for The Pick lottery. If an unusual car pulled in front of him as he drove south on I–19 headed to work at 4:00 a.m., he'd memorize the license plate. Sometimes he'd use the numbers as he saw them, and sometimes he'd add up the numbers and use those numbers instead. He'd ask coworkers how old they were or what year they were born, and used those numbers. Enraptured by a particular café customer, he'd note the number of dollars and cents on their receipt. He counted clouds in the sky and quail chicks following behind their mother. There were numbers everywhere, all day long, that never lied to him. For my father, all the numbers were sacred, revealing a story told to him personally from on high, evidence of a coincidence transformed—a mystery translated into my father's own personal truth.

———————

When the time came, I called Tony Peyron on the telephone to tell him the big news.

I'm going to get married! I shouted into the line.

What? he said without pause. *What are you gonna do that for?* He laughed like a faucet drip and for the rest of the phone call we talked about how the evaporative swamp cooler wasn't relieving the heat and how the monsoon rains would take too long to arrive that year.

Another Boda de Barbacoa

I came home for Mother's Day before the wedding to introduce my fiancé, but Ricky was in Las Vegas, my mother was alone in her apartment in a tiny California town called Manteca, and Tony Peyron was too busy to see us. He was working double shifts at the casino and only came home to sleep.

I took my husband-to-be to my aunt Susie's house that Sunday so the family could see that he was strong and tall and good, and Nana and Tata approved of my choice immediately.

Welcome to the family, my tata Alberto said, shaking his hand as I watched in wonder.

We came home again to Tucson for the wedding.

My father made barbacoa. My mother wore a dress. Nana and Tata looked on like birds perched on a mesquite tree. Ricky and his friends drank late into the night and took all the leftover wedding cake to the hotel room with them. In the morning, we ate menudo topped with lime juice, cilantro, green onions, and crushed chiltepín. We opened wedding gifts on the couch that no one was allowed to sit on.

I was told that my father cried when we drove away toward our honeymoon, a half-eaten piece of pan dulce in his hand.

A couple of years later, I brought my husband back to Tucson, this time for good. My mother came home with us. My brother too. And for a few months, we all lived crowded into my father's house on the hill untangling everything we had thrown into a pile long before. As my father says, *Everyone comes back to Tucson.*

Lunch with Sleepy

I park across the street from 77 West Washington and stare at
Sleepy from inside my car. I can't see into the windows of the old
adobe house. The dark-green roof tiles are badly weathered now.
They look like leaves about to fall from a tree. I reach my hand
into a paper bag and pull out some takeout food. I eat it alone, air
conditioning blasting. It tastes like canyon sand or like signed
pieces of paper. I chew and swallow quickly.

Leaving Menlo

Climbing out of downtown and crossing the parched Santa Cruz River again, I look up to the top of Sentinel Peak on my way into Barrio Menlo. Nana and Tata sit at the kitchen table when I arrive. They tell me about all their aches and pains, about which neighbor passed away this month. They mourn how little flavor the beef from the grocery store offers and about how the neighborhood is changing too much. I listen, but I am not there often enough to know anything beyond small talk, beyond the obvious pilfering of the barrio by all kinds of newcomers buying up homes and land next to Nana and Tata.

When I bring up the topic of a new development, Tata shakes his head and says, *They should just leave it alone. I don't like it.*

Nana sits motionless, her hair growing longer and lighter, her voice more frail than last year.

How is Ricky? she asks with each lull in the conversation.

He is good, I repeat, but I don't really know.

I remember Tata taking us to his cuartito at the edge of the yard, the edge of our world. We peek into his dark little room lined with tools and gadgets and ripped lawn chairs. On a wooden table in front of the cuartito, he slices open a catfish from Kennedy Lake, a fresh catch he hooked in the dark morning hours while we all slept. He pulls his knife out from the back pocket of his denim jeans, and we watch the insides of that fish stream out and slide across the wooden block. Ricky asks question after question. I watch without understanding torn flesh, how a head can be pulled away from a body, how simple it is to break apart a recently living thing, how effortless it is to take it out of its world and make it new in ours. Nana tends to her garden, her reptile hands grasping rusted scissors, her long, painted nails framed in dirt-covered cuticles. Nana waters the plants with the rainwater collected from the roof, spilling loud after each rain into a round tin basin. She lets us lean over the basin's rim and dunk the watering pail under the brown pool slowly until it is filled. I fight to bring the pail up from the dark water. Nana's fingers sweep over leaves like a hairbrush stroking a lock of hair that springs off a curler. Digging, scooping, pushing, and rooting, she makes even the dirt produce.

———————

In a Clorox-wiped hospital room, someone tells me about Tata's latest escape attempt. Ricky says there should be a sitter in the room with Tata, someone strong enough to keep him from pulling out the tubes and getting out of bed. Tata has escaped a few times. He is tiny and strong, and there is still a remnant of the light-weight boxer he used to be. Tata was competing in matches even after my father was born, but I only watched him watching boxing matches on TV. Seeing him now in his hospital bed, I can imagine what he looks like climbing back into the ring. Thin and tired, he has enough willpower to pull out the tubes again and again.

Nana isn't here. She is told some of this deathbed truth, but she hasn't digested all of it. She is passing through it. She forgets some names and some faces, but everyone knows she wants to be driven home, away from the hospice-care facility where Tata is slipping away.

———————

I remember mornings in Menlo. The coffeepot is hot and ready before 6:00 a.m., when my father drops us off at my nana and tata's house at 42 North Melrose Avenue. Ricky and I ritually pass through the front gate and walk up the brick path shaded by a mesquite tree on the left, a grapefruit tree on the right. We cross under the white-painted arch at the front door and knock. Kisses. Good-mornings. With Nana's hair already brushed and set and Tata's hair like a cartoon character, we parade ourselves into the kitchen. Slow moving, Nana has already been up at least an hour, and Tata has already returned from early-morning fishing, bringing with him the sun gesturing over the mountains. Nana stands at the kitchen sink, looking out the window to observe the sunrise as it reflects iridescence on each hummingbird visiting the feeder hanging on her kumquat tree. Nana is devoted to her birds. Tata ushers us out the kitchen door into the backyard, commenting on the progress of his chile seedlings along the path until we reach the patio table. Here we sit sideways on white wrought iron chairs and outline the delicate loops of the iron with our fingers, resting them on cushions of green-leafed oilcloth. Ricky is close to Tata, watching him roll cigarettes. When I promise to be careful, Nana serves me café con leche in her miniature porcelain teacup. I hold the cup and saucer carefully, making sure to not smash their painted flowers. Nana lets me pull the honey out of the honey jar with its wooden dipper, and I watch its supple gold slowly descend into my tiny cup. We splash it with milk, cool from the refrigerator, and I push my breath slowly over the brim to make tiny ripples on the surface, watching it change to creamy brown before I take a sip.

When it is Tata's time, I drive west into a setting sun toward the hospice center. Everyone is already there except my mother, my brother, me, and Tony Peyron. Tata isn't pulling out his tubes anymore. There is no escaping, no secret midnight walks to Menlo Park Liquors, no more surgeries and no more trips to the lake. When I get to his bedside, his eyes are already closed. I touch his arm. I get close to his face and whisper into his ear.

Nana sits in the patio garden beside Tata's hospice room, then after his last breath, she is taken away and medicated. I sit in the garden, in the spot where she sat. Other family members sit there too, in silence. I want Nana to come back and take a garden hose to the plants growing in that hospice patio.

Weeks or months later, my cousins find Tata's stash of whiskey in the truck parked in the backyard. The bottles swish around like liquid gold when they pull the truck out from the carport for the last time. Behind the cuartito, someone unearths the empty bottles he had buried in the shade of my graffitied nopales. When everyone is gone, I don't want to go into the house as much as I want to go into the backyard. But I don't enter. I wonder what the real estate agents and developers will think when they eventually uproot everything buried under Barrio Menlo.

———————

After our café con leche, Nana walks us through the quiet morning air. We examine her succulents dripping from hanging pots. All her plants line up and welcome the sun. She takes us into the greenhouse, where I stand in the middle of the small, hot space, wishing I had eyes like a deer, eyes big enough to see all the way around me, pushing every pot, every vine, and every small spill of soil into my field of vision. Ricky and I admire our alien skin, lime green from the reflection of the house's plastic corrugated walls, and we are transfigured. We talk differently, walk differently, and become different creatures in this second greenhouse world. Beside the carport, we run along the chain link fence, pushing on it along the way. We practice tossing pebbles into the birdbath and sweep our hands against the clean sheets Nana has hung out to dry. Ricky and I fight, then laugh like boiling pots, then fight again in a never-ending power play. By noon, it is too hot to fight, and we run into the kitchen to retrieve a soft paper towel soaked under the cold-water faucet. We squeeze the paper tight, then carefully unfold it to pull out its wrinkles. We place the cold compresses on our foreheads, cooling us as we lie limp on Nana's sofa.

In a hotel room in Chicago, I read the news on my computer screen that Nana has passed away. I dial my mother's phone number violently, like I am punching numbers through a wall.

I didn't want to bother you while you were away. I figured you were flying back in a couple days anyway. It is not like you can get here any sooner, my mother explains.

I board a plane headed west, my anger expanding like a swollen wound, and when I arrive home, Tony Peyron pulls up in his truck. He walks through my front door asking me about the weather in Chicago. He is all small talk.

Why haven't you said that Nana died? I finally yell.

Oh yeah. She did. I forgot, he pretends. I leave the room. He sits there alone in my dining room for a while before leaving too.

I had imagined Nana carried off by the birds that visited her bedroom window, like Cinderella's blue dress dancing gracefully in the breeze. Instead of floating, Nana lay on a bed or sat in a chair and evaporated away over a few years. In the days after she died, the only thing I manage to be grateful for is that she hadn't yet forgotten my name.

My family caravans through the cemetery again, following the winding path between withered grass and plastic windmills. Nana and Tata are buried side by side and Ricky and I and all our family dip our hands into dirt one last time in their presence, letting the pebbles and sand slip through our fingers.

I remember a picture. After 3:00 p.m. *Scooby Doo*, Ricky and I pluck purple trumpets from the Texas sage bush in the front yard and place them in a bowl. Nana threads the needle. Our plump fingers string the blossoms into violet bracelets, necklaces, and crowns. Nana has us kneel down in the garden on the grass, and adorned with our desert leis, we lift our chins proudly in a back-yard kingdom. Nana snaps a picture before the flowers wilt.

My father pulls up in his pickup, honking his horn, and Ricky and I kiss Nana and Tata good-bye. Driving away from 42 North Melrose, he makes his routine stop at Jeff's, a Chinese market, for his beer and our snacks. The truck winds around Sentinel Peak and my father points out the memorial crosses on the side of the mountain. We pop M&M's or Skittles, sip Coors or Coco Rico, and slowly slip into a kind of myopia. We arrive home, separate into our own rooms, and forget about black, curly bugs in soil pots, catfish scales glistening in the dawn, and milk-laced coffee cooling in miniature teacups. We forget about Nana and Tata for the rest of the night, forget about how they were growing us, slic-ing us open, and bringing us out of our sleep each morning. Our memories of them fade under the bright lights of adolescence and shrivel beneath the years spent away from Menlo. This sanctuary will lose its green and return to dust. The hummingbirds will visit other neighborhoods. When they are gone and their house is put up for sale, Ricky and I won't have enough money to buy it, so we will sulk into ourselves, into our own roots, thorns, and branches.

Beatification

FIGURE 11 Martina Perez and her nine children in front of the San Augustín Cathedral. Left to right: Soledad, Aurelia, Maria, Miguel, Juanita, Aurora (Vory), Martina, Angelita, Guadalupe, and Micaela. Photo from author's personal collection.

Blessed are the poor in spirit,
for theirs is the kingdom of heaven.

Aurelia Perez Gallego, of Tucson, passed away December 23, 1995. Preceded in death by her husband, Esteban F. Gallego. Survived by son, Steve A. (Carolina) Gallego; grandchildren, David Gallego, Lorena Gallego; sisters, Soledad Tarazon, Juanita (Alberto) Peyron, Mary (Frank) Spatafore, Angela (Armando) Peyron, Lupe, Micaela, Aurora Perez;

brother, Miguel (Carmen) Perez. Also
survived by numerous other relatives.
Visitation will be held on Thursday,
December 28, 1995 from 4:00 p.m. to 10:00
p.m. at TUCSON MORTUARY, (South Chapel), 240 S. Stone Ave., with rosary recited at 7:30 p.m. Mass will be offered
Friday at St. Augustine Cathedral at
9:00 a.m. Interment will follow at Holy
Hope Cemetery. Arrangements by TUCSON
MORTUARY, INC.

Blessed are those who mourn,

for they will be comforted.

Soledad Perez Tarazon of Tucson, Arizona, passed away March 10, 2002. Preceded in death by husband, Dolores
"Chacho" Tarazon; parents, Aurelio and
Martina Perez; sister and brother-in-
law, Aurelia and Steve Gallego. Survived by brother, Miguel (Carmen) Perez; sisters, Juanita (Albert) Peyron,
Maria (Frank) Spatafore, Angela (Armando) Peyron; Lupe, Aurora and Micaela Perez, all of Tucson. Visitation will
be held on Friday, March 15, 2002 from
4:00 p.m. to 10:00 p.m. at CARRILLO'S
TUCSON MORTUARY (South Chapel), 240
S. Stone Ave., with a Rosary recited at
7:00 p.m. Mass will be offered on Saturday, March 16, 9:00 a.m. at St. Augustine
Cathedral, 192 S. Stone. Interment to
follow at Holy Hope Cemetery. Soledad
was the owner/proprietor of El Rapido
for many years, until her retirement
in 1979. She will be missed by her family and friends. Arrangements by CAR-
RILLO'S TUCSON MORTUARY, INC.

Blessed are the meek,

for they will inherit the earth.

Angela Perez Peyron, passed away on April 30, 2003. Survived by husband Armando B. Peyron; brother, Miguel (Carmen) Perez; sisters, Juanita (Albert) Peyron, Maria (Frank) Spatafore, Lupe, Micaela and Aurora Perez all of Tucson. Rosary will be recited at St. Augustine's Cathedral, 192 S. Stone Ave., on Tuesday, May 6, 2003, 9:30 a.m. followed by Mass at 10:30 a.m. Interment will follow at Holy Hope Cemetery. Arrangements by CARRILLO'S TUCSON MORTUARY, INC.

Blessed are those who hunger and thirst for righteousness, for they will be filled.

Miguel C. (Mike) Perez born July 2, 1931 was called to his heavenly home on October 10, 2010. Mike passed away peacefully surrounded by family after a short battle with cancer. He is survived by wife, Carmen; sons and daughters-in-law, Martin and Josephine, Miguel JR and Liana, Marcos and Geraldine; grandchildren, Nicholas, Joseph, Maricela, Michael, Martina, Marcos, Alea and Diego; sisters, Lupe, Aurora and Micaela Perez, Maria Spatafore, and Juanita Peyron and many nieces and nephews. Preceded in death by parents, Aurelio and Martina Perez; sisters, Soledad Tarazon, Aurelia Gallego and Angie Peyron. After completing his service in the Navy, Mike returned to Tucson where he worked for O'Rielly Motor Company for 32 years until his retirement in 1990. Mike was a wonderful husband, parent, grandfather and friend to so many. He was enthusiastically involved in numerous civic activities and enjoyed supporting his grandchildren's many sporting, dancing and musical activities. Mike enjoyed spending time with his family

and friends listening to his favorite
Mariachi groups as well as attending
Wildcat basketball and football games
with his many close friends. Mike will
always be remembered as a kind-hearted
person and will be missed by all. Visitation will be held Sunday, October 17,
2010, 5:00 p.m-10:00 p.m. at CARRILLO'S
TUCSON MORTUARY (South Chapel) 240 S.
Stone Ave., with a Rosary recited at
7:00 p.m. Mass will be offered Monday,
October 18, 2010, 10:30 a.m. at St. Augustine's Cathedral, 192 S. Stone Ave.
Interment to follow at Holy Hope Cemetery. Arrangements by CARRILLO'S TUC-
SON MORTUARY, INC.

Blessed are the merciful,
for they will be shown mercy.

Guadalupe "Lupe" Perez was born May 26,
1923, in El Paso, Texas, but spent most
of her life in Tucson, Arizona. She was
called home on November 5, 2010. Preceded in death by parents, Aurelio and
Martina Perez; sisters, Soledad Tarazon, Aurelia Gallego, Angelita Peyron,
and brother, Miguel C. Perez. She is
survived by her sisters, Aurora and
Micaela Perez, Maria (Frank) Spatafore,
Juanita Peyron; sister-in-law, Carmen
B. Perez and many nieces and nephews. Lupe attended local schools and
graduated from Tucson High School in
1942. Lupe was secretary-treasurer of
the Alianza Hispano Americana Insur-
ance/Fraternal group for many years,
and later became executive secretary
to Dr. Bartley Cardon, President of
Arizona Feeds Company, until she retired. Lupe loved to travel, listen to
classical music, and Mariachi music
and to spend time with her many nieces and nephews in their sports, dance,
and musical activities. She will be re-

membered as a kind-hearted, generous
person and will be missed by all who
knew her. Visitation will be held Saturday, November 13, 2010, 8:30 a.m-9:30
a.m. at CARRILLO'S TUCSON MORTUARY
(South Chapel) 240 S. Stone Ave., with
a Rosary recited at 9:30 a.m. Mass will
follow, 10:30 a.m. at St. Augustine's Cathedral, 192 S. Stone Ave. Interment at
Holy Hope Cemetery. Arrangements by
CARRILLO'S TUCSON MORTUARY, INC.

Blessed are the pure in heart,
for they will see God.

Maria Perez Spatafore, beloved wife
of Frank Spatafore for 58 years, was
called home on January 28, 2012, after a long illness. Maria was born October 23, 1919 in Douglas, Arizona. She
attended local schools and graduated from Tucson High School. Maria was
a bank auditor for Southern Arizona
Bank, First Interstate Bank and Wells
Fargo Bank for 30 years until her retirement in 1982. Preceded in death by
parents, Aurelio and Martina Perez;
sisters, Soledad Tarazon, Aurelia Gallego, Angelita Peyron, Lupe Perez and
brother, Miguel C. Perez. Survived by
her husband, Frank Spatafore; sisters,
Aurora and Micaela Perez, Juanita Peyron; sisters-in-law, Carmen Perez, Marie
Belardi, Angeline Chenoweth and Gloria Block; nephew, Steve Gallego and
many other nieces and nephews. She
will be greatly missed by all who knew
her and loved her. The family requests
that in lieu of flowers a contribution
to a favorite charity be made in Maria's name. Visitation will be held on
Wednesday, February 8, 2012, 8:30 a.m.-
10:00 a.m. at St. Augustine's Cathedral,
192 S. Stone Ave., with Rosary recited
at 9:00 a.m. and Mass at 10:30 a.m. Inter-

ment to follow at Holy Hope Cemetery.
Arrangements by CARRILLO'S TUCSON
MORTUARY, INC.

Blessed are the peacemakers,
for they will be called children of God.

Juanita Perez Peyron, age 94, of Tucson,
Arizona, passed away March 25, 2012.
Preceded in death by husband, Albert
Peyron; parents, Aurelio and Martina
Perez; sisters, Soledad Tarazon, Aure-
lia Gallego, Maria Spatafore, Angela
Peyron, Lupe Perez and brother, Miguel
Perez. Survived by her children, Susan
Willhite (Buckley), Yvette Beauchamp,
Albert Peyron Jr. and Tony (Anna) Peyron; six grandchildren, James Willhite,
Celeste Malaby, Melani Martinez, Richard Peyron, Clay and Cara Beauchamp;
four great-grandchildren, Ivan, Gen-
esis, Nadya Willhite and Lola Martinez; sisters, Aurora and Micaela Perez.
Juanita was a beloved wife, mother,
sister and her greatest pleasure as
"Nana." Juanita led a simple life with
her beloved husband, Albert of 67
years until his death in 2008. Juanita cherished all that was important:
her family and her faith in God. She
adored the outdoors, the birds, and her
garden. Her role as Nana was the high-
light of her later life, never failing
to attend the many dance concerts and
sports events of her grandchildren.
She was their greatest fan! Mom, Nana,
Sister, how you will be missed by all
of us, but never forgotten. Visitation
will be held on Friday, March 30, 2012,
8:00 a.m–10:00 a.m. at CARRILLO'S TUCSON
MORTUARY (North Chapel), 204 S. Stone
Ave., with Rosary recited at 9:00 a.m.
Mass will follow, 10:30 a.m. at St. Augustine's Cathedral, 192 S. Stone Ave.
Interment at Holy Hope Cemetery. Ar-

rangements by CARRILLO'S TUCSON MOR-
TUARY, INC.

Blessed are those who are persecuted because of righteousness,
for theirs is the kingdom of heaven.

Micaela C. Perez was born on April 24,
1926 in Bisbee, Arizona. She was called
home on April 16, 2013. Micaela is survived by her sister, Aurora Perez;
sister-in-law, Carmen B. Perez; brother-
in-law, Frank Spatafore and many nieces and nephews. She is preceded in death
by parents, Aurelio and Martina Perez;
sisters, Soledad Tarazon, Aurelia Gallego, Juanita Peyron, Angelita Peyron,
Lupe Perez, Maria Spatafore and brother, Miguel C. Perez. Visitation will be
held Monday, April 22, 2013 from 8:00
a.m.-10:15 a.m. with a Rosary recited at
9:00 a.m. at CARRILLO'S TUCSON MORTU-
ARY (Center Chapel) 240 S. Stone Ave.
Mass will follow, 10:30 a.m. at St. Mar-
garet Mary Church, 801 N. Grande Ave.
Interment at Holy Hope Cemetery. Thank
you to Park Avenue Rehab and Casa de
la Luz Hospice for all their help.

Blessed are you when people insult you,
persecute you and falsely say all kinds of evil against you because of me.

Aurora "Vory" Perez was born February 27, 1929 to parents, Aurelio and
Martina Perez in Bisbee, Arizona. The
youngest of the group, she grew up in
Tucson with her siblings, Micaela Perez, Soledad Tarazon, Aurelia Gallego,
Maria Spatafore, Angela Peyron, Juanita Peyron, Lupe Perez and brother, Miguel Perez. She loved football, especially the UofA, and taught her nieces
and nephews from a young age to chant
their name when the game was on. She

enjoyed live music and could often be
found at Second Saturdays downtown
with her family. She loved to be where
the action was. She always remembered
your face and could make anyone feel
welcome. She had a lovely laugh and a
beautiful smile. She retired after 23
years of service for the City of Tucson
at the Main Library and instilled a
love of books to the children in her
family. She passed peacefully at home
with a beloved family member at her
side on the afternoon of July 10, 2021.
She is missed dearly, but her spirit
will carry on through us. Visitation
will be Wednesday, July 21, 2021, 5:00
p.m. at CARRILLO'S TUCSON MORTUARY,
Rosary will begin at 7:00 p.m. Mass will
be held on Thursday, July 22, 2021 at
10:00 a.m. at St. Augustine's Cathedral.
Interment will be held at Holy Hope
Cemetery. Arrangements by CARRILLO'S
TUCSON MORTUARY.*

Rejoice and be glad,
because great is your reward in heaven.

—*El Pensamiento*

---

* The obituaries for Aurelia Perez Gallego and Soledad Perez Tarazon
originally appeared in the *Tucson Citizen.* The obituaries for Angela Perez
Peyron, Miguel Perez, Guadalupe Perez, Maria Perez Spatafore, Juanita
Perez Peyron, Micaela Perez, and Aurora Perez originally appeared in the
Arizona Daily Star.

Ghost, Part 2

Great chunks of unique Sonoran desert are stripped away—
"peeled" is the developer's term—for parking space and fairways.
Centuries-old saguaro cacti were knocked over or dug up and sold
quietly on a burgeoning black market. . . . The original plaza is
gone. Asphalt covers ancient Indian mounds. . . . Everyone has
to have a swimming pool to fill regularly. . . . You can still walk
among old adobes, even if only law firms can afford them and buy
fresh tamales at El Rapido. . . . But Tucson has been raped. Part of
the tragedy is that it all happened without many people noticing it.
−MORT ROSENBLUM, BACK HOME, 1989

I had a dream about the Molino again, Tony Peyron says sitting at
my dining table.

Oh yeah? What were you doing?

Working. There was a line out the door and nothing was ready, he
complains.

Do you want some of the soup I made? It's real good, I offer.

I'm good, he says, but a moment later he changes his mind. *Well,
maybe just a small serving.* When I serve him, he blows ripples into
the broth and waves his hand over the bowl. *I keep dreaming, you
know. Man, I dream about my mother and father all the time,* he says.
Soledad, Angie, Mike, all of them, he says.

———

Standing in downtown Tucson on Stone Avenue, I am a block
away from the Molino house. When I walk into the Pima County
Recorder's Office, I am greeted by clerks looking up from their

computers. I'm no longer a girl on her father's errand—there are no translucent bags under my arm revealing the phantom outline of disposable forks and paper napkins. All I carry is my purse, and the county workers see that I am not delivering food. They return to their screens.

I have come to look up the deeds to the land where the Molino stands, to pulse through images of old documents and decipher the calligraphy of 1933.

The bones buried beneath the county building let out an exhale that permeates their mud crypts. The bones rest several feet below everything that we can see on Stone Avenue, north of Alameda. The bones are confirmed each time the City of Tucson decides to develop again. The story of bones is written in the daily newspaper. The bodies are found and some are moved. Under my feet, beneath thick concrete slab is a three-hundred-year-old-national cemetery. Not all the bones have been disinterred and reburied to a safer spot, so their peace is pulled out, turned over, and sifted. This creates a restlessness in the city's center. Walking the streets, we walk on their graves. Visiting the Molino's neighborhood, the Presidio, the old and evaporated fort wall, we inhale what was left of their last breaths. We forget what they called their own. We forget their lives, what they sang, and what they ate.

I set my purse down at a desk with a computer screen. I can hear a man arguing with a clerk, insisting on his mother's ownership of some remote property. I haven't much to go on. I search the address 220 North Meyer. I scan lists of handwritten documents. There are bills of sale. There are intersections and dates. But whatever it is I am looking for in these pages of history is cut off to me, like the edges of an atlas. Like the jagged frame of Tito's photos on rocks. I see a few names attached to the address: Helen Aboud, Honan and Bessie Thomas, Carmen de Pacheco, William and Phoebe Pearce, May M. Clarke and Annie Marsteller. The list goes on, reaching back to somewhere around the year 1900, before statehood and before the Santa Cruz River ran dry. I mouth their names into the air between me and the screen. A vapor settles.

My best guess is that the building, the Molino house where my grandmother grew up, must have been built around the arrival of the railroad, in the 1880s. A Sonoran transformation of mud bricks next to the river and between the mountains. I stand up from the desk. I wait in line. When my number is called, I ask the clerk to print out the deeds for me, and I keep them in my purse as I walk out into the sun wondering where we come from.

When I climb into the car with my mother, I tell her how I spent my day.

Why are you looking this up? she asks. *I don't understand. What does it matter?*

I don't understand what kind of question she is asking, so I say, *I want to find out when the Molino was built*, as though that is a reasonable response.

These documents will only show the deeds to the property. They won't tell you when it was built. Don't you know that? They could have been buying and selling just the land, not the house.

Her words make me a fool who spent hours sitting in the recorder's office as though I belonged there. I lie to her, and pretend, because I don't know how to say what I'm really looking for. She won't understand, I decide. This isn't something I can say in casual conversation, in between slurps of fideo soup, or sitting in the passenger seat of a minivan on our way to Walmart. This is not how we talk. There is no way to say what microfilm deeds will offer me. There is no way to say that lately I am feeling empty. No way to blame her or my father or their mothers or fathers. There is no way to ask if there is something wrong with me wanting a good ghost story.

You don't believe in ghosts, she says.

I can't be the only one to walk into a government building looking for answers on notarized certificates, I say to myself.

I imagine the loops in cursive letters on the deeds in my purse. I think of how much the ground beneath us doesn't belong to us, and how reconciliation feels as far away as my days kneeling in church before a priest. I eat words and change the subject and we settle into the drive toward another discount shopping spree.

———————

The Molino sits on the edge of a Tucson fortress, flanked by burial sites of Spanish militia and Hohokam pit houses planted a long time ago. Bodies covered in lime powder are laid out to magnetic east and west. Alameda Street was once called Cemetery Street, and downtown Tucson is built on bodies. We don't know their names and we don't know what belongs to them. No documents identify them or what they owned. The fort wall is gone. My father's Molino is gone. *No one died in the old house,* my nana used to say, and I can hear her voice long after she is gone. *Mijita, you don't have to worry because it is not haunted,* she assured me over and over. I am disappointed over and over. I keep asking Tony Peyron if he ever had a ghost experience in the old house, hoping he will remember something—give me some bit of information I have never heard before about us, about them, about what is gone. Though Tony Peyron is the teller of all kinds of ghost stories, though he is the kind of man that makes spirits out of light reflections and alien sightings out of stars, though I've heard every kind of absurd tale he's told to attentive children, he never claims to have seen a ghost in the old house. But his stories eventually contradict my nana Juanita's words. He says he remembers sitting in the zaguan with her and with Tito when his grandmother died in the bedroom of the old house.

He changes the subject abruptly, tells me he remembers the Aboud family. He retells a story he heard, that the Abouds had a hard time selling the building to anyone before my great-grandfather Aurelio came along. The records I've seen, the ones I keep folded in my purse or copied on a computer file all show that no one lived in the house for very long before Aurelio. New residents switched in and out every year or two for decades. Restless. My father says, *But my grandfather Aurelio was the first person to bite.*

I find that my searching doesn't quench anything at all. I keep feeling hunger and thirst, all while grasping at whatever is in front of me. I reach my hands into the dark, trying to touch something, anything. What makes plaster heads suddenly crash to the floor? What makes lightbulbs flicker and sway? What is making that noise? What is hidden from me, covering its face?

Dig

Pues, mijita,
¿cómo te llamas
tú?

Let me tell you a ghost story.

One of the bodies beneath your pueblo
was a child six years old.
Her hands are clasped.

The archeologists know why.

They have measured the depths of graves
but I am
the one who can raise them up.

De veras

no more decay
no more holes in the chest
no more oxidizing green
growing on mijita's neck twisting
strands of copper
in my shape
no more sewers beneath your feet
lined with the dead
nor soldiers nor raids
on evaporated presidios.

Flesh gives birth to flesh
but the Spirit gives birth to spirit.

Birth comes with names
pero no te preocupes.

I will dig out a new name for you
and we will carve it together in stone.

—*El Pensamiento*

Sold

After meeting him a few times, Tony Peyron decided Alex was *a real good guy, you know what I mean?* Alex was the man who purchased the whole property that was the Molino and my great-grandfather's house. I don't know exactly who owned and sold the property, but at the time, we assumed that he bought it from my uncle Mike's widow, Aunt Carmen, and their three sons. My father visited Alex often while he was renovating the adobes and had long conversations about God knows what. Alex was an artist, a teacher, a kind and gentle voice who had recently received an inheritance from his mother and his partner. He was excited to share the potsherds from beneath the floorboards with my dad. He was ready to talk about ghosts. I also met him by chance, a few blocks from the Molino, and we talked for a while. He was a willing listener. He mentioned that one of the renovation workers, ironically also named Tony, had felt a presence while working in the building, but, Alex said, *Tony didn't want to get into it*, which sounded familiar to me so I didn't press him for more.

I was curious about Alex, and I imagine he was curious about me and my family, so he seemed to be the right person to admit some things to. Because my father assured me he was *a real nice guy*, I admitted to Alex I had been scared to go into the house.

Places are scary because of our personal traumas, he said, *and the earth remembers.*

His words were so strange to me, but also put me at ease. Alex shared that my father was not the only one coming by the Molino to see what he was up to. My uncle Tito had come with a hand-shake and a few stories. A man with a metal detector came several times and even snatched a coin he unearthed at the property before Alex could see it. My nana's last living sister, Tía Vory, came too. Alex mentioned that Vory had called my father a thief, that Tony Peyron could not be trusted.

Yeah, you know my nephew, Tony? He took everything and the front door, she told Alex. The front door part was true. Decades before, he had commissioned a local blacksmith to make the security door for him, welding "El Rapido" into the iron. The blacksmith often traded work with my father—welding for tamales. He had even crafted the Argentine wheeled parrilla in our front yard. After the Molino closed, Tony Peyron considered the door his own, so he brought it home. He hung it as an entrance into his makeshift garden next to the parrilla.

I told Alex, *Tony Peyron has been accused of many things.* I told him the story about how, recently, some family members had arranged to see Tony Peyron in Menlo to ask him about all his crimes. In a heated exchange, they accused Tony Peyron of keeping a key to the Molino so that he could go in and steal kitchen equipment. I told Alex how I heard about it later from my aunt Susie. She said my father was hot with anger about the Menlo ambushing, about the accusations. She said he came to her house in tears.

Tony Peyron is no saint, I told Alex, but I had never seen these particular crimes. Lots of sad things happen to families after Molinos die, I guess.

I guess it runs in the family, I said. *I'm a thief too, you know. I feel a little guilty for taking things out of the house, stealing from it, when I was just a kid.*

Nothing belongs to anyone, Alex replied.

Inviting me into the house, Alex wanted me to see the building's bare bones during renovation, and though it felt strange, I took him up on the offer. It was the first time I got to stand in the room that used to be my nana's beauty salon. It had been locked away my whole life. For the first time, I saw that the ceiling was falling down in that room, the only space in the house that was flat roofed and not covered by the pyramidal roof of the territorial-style home. Through a big hole in the rotted roof of Nana's salon,

I stared at a swath of blue sky for as long as I could. I told Alex that my family said Nana's name was removed from any inheritance documents even before she passed away. I wasn't sure if that was true, but I knew she didn't get her salon. As we stood in that room, I felt the need to describe Nana to him, how she was such a good cook, how she could make plants grow and how she was so cariñosa. I remember I used a word to describe her that didn't make sense at first. It was a word that fit her and also didn't fit her, a word that describes a person bearing a burden or someone who holds their strength under control.

Of all the Perez sisters, I think my nana was the meekest, I said to Alex.

The meanest? he asked.

No, the meekest, I shouted, laughing like a little busted water sprinkler.

Oh, meekest! he said. *Well you know, the meek shall inherit the earth.*

Inheritance

After the Molino was sold, our family only visited the Presidio a couple more times together. Once, we visited the Spring Arts Festival at the Tucson Museum of Art, an excuse to go back and see who and what was there in our places. The Molino's exterior had been repainted, the insides gutted, but the Sleepy Mexican remained. Alex kept a little art gallery in its place for a short while, but then subleased the property to others, the house as an Airbnb and the Molino as a boutique pasta shop. This fate matched the new look of the neighborhood. The art festival around the corner boasted tables of decadent croissants, berry muffins, and cake pops. There were clean, modern lines welcoming tourists. There were booths selling glazed pottery, newly crafted jewelry, and paintings of coyotes on the desert horizon. And I was confused by my feelings there among the food crafts and artisans. One moment, I felt so attracted to their wares, their rich spreads. The next moment, I wanted to toss their tables over and chase the vendors out with a bundle of yucca leaves.

My father was hesitant at first, walking into the entrance of what was once El Rapido, now renamed and rearranged. We immediately noticed several antique-framed black-and-white portraits hung on the walls. They were unfamiliar faces, a family that was not ours. We found lavish grocery products too. My father gawked at everything in the room, nervously shifting his weight. After his reluctance to go in, it now seemed my father didn't know how to walk out again. We could not stay. I tried to keep calm, but it felt as though something quaked inside the Molino, and a thunder rolled in my ears. I watched my father slowly step out the front door and back into the sun on Washington. I took out my camera phone and snapped his picture next to the Sleepy Mexican.

We walked through the arts festival grounds like spectators at a sport we didn't know how to play. Then we left.

On the drive home, I broke down. Convinced that no other living souls in my family cry over these things, I comforted myself by deciding to just accept it: weeping is my inheritance.

A Letter from My Woke Corn Sister

Dear Sleepy,

Wake up! Wake up and spread the radical mestiza feminist
epistemology! Wake up, cabrón! Don't you know we've been
colonized? Don't you know Western capitalism is coursing
through the veins of every Euro and U.S. centrist hell-
bent on destroying cultura indígena, excluding the peoples
differentiated, our peoples, our histories, our traditions, our
culinary contributions, in favor of their imperialist narratives
that want to keep us drunk and lazy on posters but sober and
overworked on the rancho, in the fields, in the back kitchen—
way back—all the way back behind a thick wall painted with
hyper-tropical colors, swinging piñatas, sombreros filled with
free-flowing margaritas and nacho cheeze?! Wake up! Your
ancestors are calling you, Pancho. You've been anglicized, Pedro.
You've been duped and brown-faced, Maria mía. Pues, ándale,
Speedy Gonzales! ¡El Rapido! ¡El flojo! ¡El borracho! ¡Ya, pues!
Who do you think you are, sleeping there, qué estúpido, leaning
on cactus thorns? Letting yourself be pierced? How dare you
linger here with your blanket like everything is fine, like there
isn't a storm ready to drown us all, a sea of hatred ready to
capsize us? Wake up! Can't you feel the boat rocking, pendejo?
¡Apúrate, güey! There is no rest here! How dare you rest? Can't
you see, can't you hear, these chains on the necks of your people!
Wake up! Don't you care? Don't you care if we drown? Help us!
For Chrissake. Why do you hide your face from us? Wake up
and help us! Help us. Help.

—Tu hija

Gethsemane

Sea,
peace be with you.

Wind,
be still.

Come
down the mount
to the press with me.

Sit
while I pray
y watchate.

Watch me
not hiding
my distress from you.

Look at me
when I plead
for any other way around this,
God please,

remember
I feel you.

When I find your eyes
your limbs
heavy
I will tell you,

Wake up
y vamos.

—*El Pensamiento*

The Creature

My corn sister told me a ghost story about a sad traveler she met once by the dry river. She said they called him Julián Gonzalez or Luis Romero Soto or Victor Something or Other. The man claimed to be ripped from the inside out by a desire to save his mother from the evil metate that lived in her kitchen.

Whatever his name was, he told my corn sister that his mother belonged to a long line of women who knelt before the metate each day. The metate was a blanched volcanic rock that a friend of the family had pulled from the belly of some ancient beast, but no one knows the beast's name anymore. It was a beaten stone, blackened and pockmarked. A very weighty subject. The man didn't fully trust the metate, but it didn't matter because it was only there for his mother.

Each morning before dawn, before the mother's eyes were fully open, before café con leche and before she had a chance to remember the impossible things she dreamed about the night before, his mother bent down before the metate. This meeting provided a wealth of the best tortillas anyone in the man's home had ever tasted. This metate and this mother, their daily genuflections, had made everything else going on in this crazy world bearable.

From generation to generation, women leaned into this pressing power, a mighty millwork over the metate. Thinking it was an unfortunate burden on her, the man pitied his poor mother at work over the metate. He claimed he sought her relief, but my corn sister could see the lie under his tongue. There festered his quiet fantasy: a bitter end to the metate. My corn sister had already noticed this seed of jealousy growing out of his mouth and trickling down his chin, how he longed to be in place of the metate, the object of his mother's endless caresses each morning and baths each evening.

The man had been scribbling his plans on amate paper for years and was finally ready to mold the creature that would bring an end to the metate. It would be made of metal and it would control every mother's kitchen in the world. The man's plan would bring a revolution, it would bring him fame and fortune, and finally he would have his mother's attention. Each day, the man's belly and chest grew swollen with the pride of having conceived this greatness.

The man schemed, trying again and again to manufacture his masterpiece with a part galvanized steel, a part molten metal, a beam forged in iron. But his experiments failed time after time. Vexed and sullen, he cried out to Moloch or Ba'al or Tlaloc and pleaded for success until the answer finally came to him in a prayer-drunken stupor. He lacked a kind of power, like a bolt of lightning.

Since the only power anyone had in his tiny village was the nearby mouth of the volcano, which would surely bring him to the brink of suicide, he devised instead a plan to steal his mother's metate. To take its power.

One night while she slept, using every drop of his anger as fuel, he lifted the heavy metate and slammed it against iron until it was a shape he found more dignified and worthy of technological sophistication. He lifted his creation up and ignited it with electricity until, behold, a fierce machine was wrought. In a fit of joy at his success, he shouted out the window to the sleeping tiny town, "Worry not, my pueblito named for a water baptizer, for I shall develop not only my fine invention, but also a vast company of power; it shall be called the Malinche Corporation, and it will flood the land with this machine until every last mother, bent and bowing before metate, can finally be free!"

That same night, the man fell delightfully asleep in new moon darkness, but all his efforts were in vain. As he dreamt in slumber, the machine he had made left his side, slithered into his mother's bedroom, climbed into her mind, and there murdered her spirit.

When the man awakened to find his mother empty and pale, he fled. He feared at first his fall from fame, but then feared more the machine he had made. He feared it would hunt him down and steal his soul too.

My corn sister says that the man fled his pueblito, his state, his homeland, and finally came to our dry river. There she watched him weep, remorseful and broken, and the image of him slowly brought compassion enough to keep my corn sister's heart from climbing a high tower wall and dropping a great millstone on his head.

Pool Baptism

There is a room beneath the surface of the water in the neighborhood pool where I will be baptized as an adult. It is a room flooded with light.

When I tell my parents that I am going to be baptized, my mother says, *Again?*

My father says, *What for?*

But they both come to this second baptism. They watch my body float into the water room of a pool that they have never entered.

I don't remember what is said to me the moment before I go under the water, when I am plunged into that room. I think I'm supposed to remember. But it is as far away to me now as the moment of my infant baptism.

In the room, there are other bodies. They swirl fleshy but unburdened by their weight.

They don't stay long.

This is not a room for sitting or grinding stones or collecting dust. The walls sway and the floor bobs up and down. There are no doors but many windows. There are no hallways from this room to that. There is no piano down in the water and no cats pawing at the keys.

I'm here in this room because I RSVP'd.

I'm breathless. I feel a push and pull, but no sting. My body is soft and limp and my hair dances around my face. All the fire there is quenched.

When I leave the room, someone's hand is on my back, guiding me to underwater stairsteps. My parents look on with curiosity and confusion. I drip with remnants of the room. A towel wrangles me out. There are many days between this one and when I will return, but I am given a vision of a household, a family of many flooded rooms. A place prepared for me.

Sobremesa

On the table there is salsa and fresh corn chips. On its way is a crisp tortilla sobaquera covered in melted cheese. My father motions with his whole body to the waiter at the other end of the dining room and my mother shakes her head in embarrassment.

We wanna order! We're ready! he shouts at the waiter.

No we aren't! my mother and brother shout in unison.

Just one more minute, I say to the waiter and he smiles and jumps to his next task.

Why do you do that? my mother asks.

What? my father says, and lifts his eyebrows high like the question is more shocking than his harassing the waiter. *I'm ready man. I'm hungry!*

Eat some chips, Ricky says.

I don't want to fill up on chips, my father says. *I'm trying to lose weight. Eat healthy. Come on, man. I don't wanna be heavy. Didn't you see whatshername at the party yesterday? Man, she's this big,* he says as he stretches his arms out wide like he's holding a hoop around that tortilla sobaquera.

Stop it, I say. *Why do you have to say things like that, huh? She's not even that big. And anyway, look at you—you aren't skinny.*

I'm not like THAT, he says and holds the extra-wide sobaquera again.

When I tell him to stop, I wonder how many of these things he has said to me as a child. How much have I forgotten?

What about me, huh? I point to my stomach and my father hides his face behind one hand to protect himself from the look of me. Ricky laughs like a sputtering steam valve, but I don't want to laugh this time. I call the waiter back and order a margarita with salt.

A few hours earlier, we were standing four or five blocks from the Molino in the south parking lot of the cathedral, the "mother" church of the Roman Catholic Diocese of Tucson. It had just been renovated, but didn't look new to me. As we got out of the car, my brother pulled his belted pants up and shifted his button-down shirt. *I hate this*, he said.

No one likes funerals, I said, unsure if he was complaining about the formal clothes or the Mass we were about to attend.

On the cathedral's façade, yucca, saguaros, and nopales gather around coats of arms and crosses, and a horned lizard sits alert. Inside the sanctuary, the ceiling, stained glass, and painted plaster walls loomed over our heads. We sat and stood, kneeled, and kneeled again before the altar and the draped coffin. I could hear Ricky huff each time the priest spoke. His words repeated in my mind: *I hate this. I hate this.*

The Mass ended and as we walked back to the parking lot, he said, *This is so crazy. The whole time I was thinking, what are we doing? Why are we doing this? This is a cult.*

It had been a while since Ricky had stepped into a church, since the last funeral, but I know that routine was not lost on him. After the ceremony, we caravaned to Holy Hope Cemetery to attend the burial. We huddled near the only ramada canopy over the grave in the hottest part of the day, the sun wicking away our sweat. We said our good-byes quickly to get back into air-conditioned vehicles. Everyone hurried to go eat. Eating is what we do after we've lost something.

My father sits up in his seat, eyes wide following the waiter's every move back and forth to the kitchen until finally he arrives with a tray of our plates: taco salad, chimichanga, chile relleno, enchiladas. Already full of chips and cheese crisp, I ask the waiter to bring more salsa.

I hate when the priest pretends to know the person who died, Ricky says.

Maybe he did know her, I say.

Yeah, right, he says, shaking his head. *Brainwashed.*

What do you mean, brainwashed?

We were brainwashed, he says.

I look up from my plate to see my mother's reaction, to see if she is offended, but Ricky's words don't seem surprising to her.

Mom, do you think we were brainwashed? I ask. *I mean, you are the one who insisted on Catholic school.*

My mother shrugs, her palms in the air. *I just thought it was better. You were gonna learn some morality, you know? It was a good school.*

Well, you went there too, I say. *You should know. They never answered questions. I started asking them by the time I was eight or nine years old. Nine years old, I remember. Third grade, Mrs. Whatshername. I told her I wasn't sure I believed in God. No one had a good answer for my questions. And in Mass we were not allowed to ask! I don't think they even wanted us to read the Bible.*

Because you probably wouldn't understand it, she says. *They didn't want you to misinterpret.*

I think I was about eleven years old, Ricky says. *I remember Nana was going to church every day at that time. And I remember she came home one time real proud of the priest.*

What? I say.

Yeah, he says laughing, *she was proud that the priest had won an argument. A stranger had come in—a man who wasn't ever there before. The priest was in the middle of the homily when this guy started yelling out questions like "Where did life come from? Where did the stars come from? Where did atoms come from?" and stuff like that. Interrupted the whole mass, Nana said. But she was proud because the priest had an answer for every question.*

What was the answer? my mother asks.

It was so stupid. He laughs again. *"God." That was it. That's all he said, and Nana thought it was so great. I mean, I was only a little kid, but I knew that was a dumb answer. Nana was proud of something that was nothing.* Ricky stops to take a big bite of his red chile chimichanga, enchilada style with a spoonful of sour cream on top. *People don't change their minds,* he says, his mouth full.

I sweep a few grains of salt off the rim into my drink with my finger. I want to talk about changing, about why I believe in something that I hadn't believed in before—a sense that grace was real—to say that I am awake with a hope that still doesn't make sense to me, but I don't have the words I want in my mouth. I keep chewing instead.

We finish our plates and sit there for another hour, talking and remembering. My father doesn't engage much except to ask us to repeat what he can't hear us say. Then Ricky says something—a joke about religious people I now don't remember exactly. I only remember my anger.

———————

I'm not Catholic! I'm not religious, I shout a little too loud in the dining room.

Whatever, he says.

I'm against religion! I say, fork in my hand. *Because Jesus was against religion!* but my words don't make sense and my pride is too big for the words anyway.

My mother doesn't say anything and my father leans back in his chair, staring at the murals of colonial Mexico painted on the walls. I put down the fork. It takes me a while to calm down and realize I haven't said the right thing. I haven't explained myself.

Ricky is better at it. He says, *You were the one who showed me. You were the one who taught me that all that stuff was a lie. Then, after we hadn't seen each other for a while, I said something, I don't remember what I brought up, but I said something against religion and you were like . . . you were saying the exact opposite! I was like, what the fuck?*

The waiter interrupts, handing us the bill, and we fall silent. I finish the bottom of my margarita and Ricky opens his phone to stare at the screen. My mother gets her wallet out. My father starts to close his eyes, fading into the first signs of a tiny food coma.

Just Asking

1. Will worrying
add a single day to your life?

2. Why are you
anxious about your body?

3. Do you believe I can do this?
3a. Are you terrified?

4. Why do you doubt?

5. How many loaves
do you have?

6. Do you not understand?

7. What do you want me to do for you?

8. Why are you testing me?

9. Could you not stay awake even one hour?
9a. Who do they say I am?
9b. Who do you think I am?

10. Why are you thinking those things
that you think in your heart?

11. Why are you weeping?
11a. Do you see anything?

12. Where is your faith?

13. Mijita, do you know your name? Who gave it to you?
13a. Who are you?

14. If even the smallest things are beyond your control,
why are you anxious about the rest?

15. Who is greater: the one seated at the table
or the one who serves?

16. Have you anything here to eat?

17. What are you looking for?

18. Do you want to be well?

19. Why are you seeking praise from others and not my praise?

20. Where can we buy enough food?

21. Does this shock you?

22. Woman, has no one condemned you?

23. If I tell the truth, why do you not believe me?

24. Aren't there twelve hours in a day?

25. Have I been with you so long and still you don't know me?

26. Who are you looking for?

27. Do you love me?

—*El Pensamiento*

Salt

My father raises some old wood posts, plywood, and a dilapidated green tarp in the corner of his desert property. He constructs a ramshackle ramada to house his cement-brick altar—a concrete table with an arched nicho adorned with misshapen prayer candles, glassless framed pictures, plastic and ceramic crosses, and soiled artificial roses in dollar store vases, things that people have thrown away. He wraps the sides of this new ramada with chicken wire. He builds six or seven short raised beds lined in aloe vera shoots. At the entrance, he makes a doorframe to hold the old wrought iron Molino door, the one with the words "El Rapido" welded into the metal. This is my father's new garden, a new place to occupy his energies. He visits the garden several times a day, starting early in the morning. He digs in the dirt, waters it with an old five-gallon paint bucket, and talks to himself there among the trash relics. It becomes as routine as the grinder, so I begin to wonder if this is my father's ofrenda to the Molino, a way to pray and spin out little holy thoughts throughout the day, like a molino reborn.

As I arrive at his west-side home, I don't have time to get out of my car before he starts telling me the news, the story, the latest. *You know I planted some carrots and beets in my garden,* he says, rubbing the dirt from his hands on his faded T-shirt. *I put some real good soil, you know? Come take a look.*

He leads me to the garden entrance and we stand there, glowing green in the shade of the worn tarp.

Hey, let me explain something to you, OK? I was walking out of the garden the other day, OK, and I saw TWO. HUGE. RATS. They ran up the side of the wall. Just like that! He mimics rat feet with his fingers crawling up the air. I scowl.

The rats hide out in the decrepit 1968 Chevy Nova that my brother has abandoned in my parents' front yard. It was the car they drove when they were first married and it has been passed around for a few decades. Ricky is the Nova's latest owner and has relinquished it to a patch of desert alongside the patio wall. Under the hood, the rats find a dark place to hide from the rattlesnake in their midst. Their long, pink tails curl around nuts and bolts. They make a home out of a motor that no longer shrugs, out of cracking wires, and vessels emptying of any remnant fluids. These are not the rodents of the city feasting on dumpster shrimp tails and asparagus tips. These are desert rats.

Man, I put so much work into my little garden. And for what? Nothing. They eat it all, those dirty rats. My father scratches his itch. Everything seems to be against him in this new labor. The desert is hostile. The soil is not good enough, and the plastic containers catching the monsoon rain from the roof run dry before the season's end. The sun beats down on every swath of leaf and tender bud. Even when the plants produce, the creatures in his yard scoop up every worthless vegetable. For some reason, it doesn't bother my father when certain animals eat. He speaks fondly of the javelinas and their babies that look like tiny ruddy puppies. He loves the white-winged doves. He has even named the field mice and coyotes. But the rats are never welcomed.

Two of those dirty rats ate the poison I put out, he says. *I found them halfway stuck in the chicken wire. You know, I had to use a hatchet to get them out.*

Oh God, Dad, I say as I cover my face.

What? They were already kinda dry. I mean, you know, they had been dead for a while already. How else was I gonna get them out? He laughs like a carbonated water burp.

I picture those little rats chopped in half, the splinter of bone and morsel of carrot stuck in their teeth, the poison trapping them before they can escape to the bowels of a dumped vehicle. I think of all the times I've tried to run away too, holing up, piling up my deadly prize. I see myself in the garden. And there is distress; there is poison and deception and food and hatchets. I cower into these thoughts for a moment, until I can walk away.

My father follows behind, still talking. *I'm not gonna weigh myself until the end of the month*, he says. *I want to lose twenty-five to thirty-five pounds. I'm supposed to be one sixty-five for my age and height, you know that? I can name you thirty-five guys from Menlo who have died: Bebo, Diego, Leo Jacobs, all those guys. I mean, come on. I don't want to suffer. I don't wanna die like that. I gotta do something. You know what I mean? I gotta do something.*

He shows me the latest book that he rescued from a dumpster. This one is thicker than most: *Our Earth, Our Cure*. I roll my eyes. He shows me the inscription on the first page. *Dear Nina* . . . something scribbled that I can't read . . . *Love, Nelida*. He explains that it is a personal note from the author, a note that seems to build credibility for my father, but the names don't match. No matter. He points to the picture of the author on the back cover—a face he can trust.

I went to that machine they have at Safeway, you know the one. That thing that measures your blood? he says. *I got prehypertension.*

High strung since forever, my father struggles to sit still long enough to explain what he thinks is the writing on the wall. Sometimes it seems like he's forgotten that something is coming for all of us, like that big yellow bulldozer. Already the world he knew is gone and health books from 1974 are being thrown in the trash, so time is running out. The inked signatures are fading and the body is giving way.

Stay away from fats, he says. *Stay away from flour, carbs, sugar, salt*, he counts on his fingers. *The worst one is salt*, he says.

Some things I know about salt: masa doesn't taste like much without it; too much can ruin a whole pot; salt in the palm of the hand feels like holding ocean air; salt kills the weeds in the garden; salt preserves and purifies. Somewhere in the Bible it says *salt is good*.

Oh, I forgot to tell you, I put the barbacoa in the pit last night, he says.
Oh yeah? I say.
You know my buddy Alejandro?
No, I don't know him.
You know! Alejandro! He says to cook the meat without salt so it stays juicy. You can always salt it after, he says. *I did it different this time. I didn't salt the meat before. Boy, is that meat tasty. I put about twenty bulbs of ajo and some oregano.* He walks over to the refrigerator and pulls out a plastic bin with some of the meat. *Here, taste it,* he says, plunking the plastic bin in front of me. He takes the first bite. *Man,* he says, holding his finger and thumb together, *just right!*

I rest the cold, salted barbacoa on my tongue. I picture a hot plate piled with rice, beans, salsa de chile verde. A folded flour tortilla and a plastic fork. I taste the smoke. I squish the tallow between my fingers. I savor it for only a few seconds before another stupid thought pops into my head: *I am too fat to eat.*

The thought sits low inside me at first. When I think of other thoughts like these, thoughts like *This makes me look fat,* or *I wish I could cut this piece off,* or *I am too fat to go to the beach,* I can hardly hold them long enough to see what they are. This time, something chases the thought to the top of my throat. I get still and keep it there. I hold it until I realize that someone told me a lie and I believed it. I still think these stupid thoughts, and sometimes they cover me like a blanket of lies.

My father takes another bite with his fingers and says, *My grandfather made more barbacoa then you can shake a stick at, you know that?*

Oh yeah? I say, reaching for another morsel of meat.

He used to cook the meat in my dad's backyard, you know, in the tinas. He used to stack the tinas up, some with barbacoa and some with nixtamal. He worked so many hours, you know what I mean? He used to shred all the meat by hand.

That's crazy, I say.

Did I tell you where we used to cater sometimes? The Phoenix High-way? Look, he says drawing in the air, *as you go on the Phoenix Highway, there was a little water trough where the water ran by the road. There were a million trees and picnic tables along that water. The City of Tucson's catered parties were out there. We had these tables with all this food and my brother, Tito, and I would be serving barbacoa, beans, and rice. I don't know how my grandfather fit that much food in the Plymouth! Food for a hundred and some people, man!*

Wow, I say with his food in my mouth.

A lot of his parties he had barbacoa. Then later in the night? The menudo would come out! He'd drive back and forth with the pots. He did so many parties. Hundreds of weddings. His stuff was good, man. He was a great cook.

My father stands and puts the bin away, back in the refrigerator. *I gotta get some water,* he says, *I've been talking too much.*

I watch him drag his feet across the kitchen floor as he goes out the door to check on the javelinas that rest in the shade of a palo verde tree on the other side of his patio wall. *They are starving, pobrecitos,* he says, reaching for a bag of crumbs.

I won't tell him not to feed the animals anymore, like I used to. I've tried to convince him that his food is bad for them, that he needs to stop, but *they are starving,* he says. He doesn't hear my voice. He doesn't listen. He goes and tosses week-old bread, limp lettuce, and a slice of cold pizza over the wall. *They eat everything,* he says.

I am not on a diet like my father. I am not looking for a medicinal cure-all for whatever is wrong with me or anyone else. I eat too much, I think. Also, I don't know what I mean when I say *too much.*

My Food

Your cravings
won't be
put up
in cupboards
in storehouses
in five-gallon drums.
Your pot will not boil in vain.
Your table is to be set night and day.

I am not a measuring tape around your waist.

I am
the temple
I came eating and drinking
I came fasting and praying
and I am the bread and I am the wine
I am the lamb
forever
I am
and my food is to do the will of the One
who sent me.

—*El Pensamiento*

El Mecapal

Under a mesquite tree canopy in his front yard, my uncle Tito leaned on two walking sticks, one in each hand. He wore a folded red bandana tied around his forehead. His little dogs ran back and forth in the yard, stirring up the dirt. There were feathers everywhere. I gave him a hug and he gave me a metal folding chair to sit in the shade of the tree. We talked about the weather first, and I asked how he was feeling. He told me about the two pieces of rawhide he was preparing for a powwow drum. He talked about the mesquite beans that needed to be collected so he could make flour. He had already broken the flagstones for photographic emulsion that morning and had to wait three more hours before he could apply the second coat, so it was a good time to visit and ask him questions. I asked if he knew about the first person to ever create the image of the Sleepy Mexican.

No, he said, *you know I got that image off of the receipt book that belonged to my grandfather. Your father called him Mr. Rapido.* He laughed. *Yeah, painting is rare for me, you know, and I remember not everyone liked it. I didn't think anything about it, myself, but other people—they didn't like it. I don't know. In México, way back, they had a rest in the afternoon. People there, they would take a break and then go back to work.*

Siesta, I said.

That's right. I just thought it was that. I didn't think there was anything wrong with it. You know, it is like something you wish for when you have to work hard; you are hoping for a little rest. Tito smiled and it reminded me of my nana. *I remember working at the Molino. When they brought in a quarter cow, I'd go in to help cut the meat. A thousand tiny pieces,* he said. *I helped make the tortillas. I sat at the end of the ramp, you know, of the tortilla machine.*

That was my first job too, I said.

I remember all the tortillas that came out with an irregular fold—they went to the family for our meals. We were eating the profit! he said, resting his hand on his stomach. *I used to hang out in the beauty shop too. I remember that smell of that stuff they used on the ladies' hair, you know those smelly chemicals, and those old hair dryers—they looked like they were from another planet. I used to put my head under those dryers and pretend I was in outer space.* He laughed, then looked down at the dirt. *I don't know why my mother stopped the beauty shop. I know she regretted it. She'd say, "By now, I'd have people working for me."* I suppose that's right too. Maybe she would have had a rest.* One of Tito's dogs, the one he calls Petunia, rested in the dust, panting at his feet, and he leaned over to tap the dog on its head. *I miss my mother,* he said. *I miss my dad too . . . all our hunting trips together. You know, I remember one time my grandfather came with us. He wasn't much into hunting, but I'll never forget it.*

Your grandfather Aurelio?

Yes, he came and surprised us all. I remember because someone shot a deer. I don't remember who, I know it wasn't me, and Grandfather offered to carry it back to camp. He must have still been physically fit at that time. And you know? I've never seen anyone carry a deer like he did.

Oh really?

*Usually, we would put the deer over our shoulders, or drag it, you know. If we were lucky, we'd have someone take it back on horseback. But my grandfather tied the feet together first. Then he got a long piece of cloth—*Tito stretched his arms out a bit, still managing to lean on the walking sticks—*and I think a belt, like a leather strip. He put the deer inside a circle of fabric and strapped the belt on to it. Then he squatted down into the circle and slung the strap across his forehead. He stood up and walked with the deer on his back like that all the way to camp! It's true! We watched him do it and we were so impressed. He had some years on him already, but he was still strong. He was a big guy, you know. I mean, they really knew how to work hard. I know women used* *to tie things like that too to their heads. They could carry such a heavy load. I wish I had my camera when I saw him do that.*

You took some good pictures, though. I've seen the one with Tata looking out over the mountains with his rifle, I said.

Yeah, you know he was reluctant when I asked him to pose for that picture, he said. The birds in the mesquite began to chirp loud over us then. *But I always wanted to photograph him out there scouting or hunting.*

My father told me that a lot of times the meat was gonna carry the family through the winter. It wasn't just for fun, I said.

I know they had it hard. Well, since I was born paraplegic, you know. Now they call it cerebral palsy.

I have a picture of Tata and my dad hunting, one you took, I think. But didn't another photograph get published in the newspaper too? That one of them carrying a big fish? I asked.

That was by the ocean. Yeah, Tony was always there hunting and fishing with my dad. He was strong too, you know. But I was kinda mean to him when we were boys.

Really? Did you fight? Like me and Ricky?

Well, I apologized to him a few years ago for that. I think what it was—I was angry because I had my disability and you know, there was nothing wrong with Tony. I took it out on him. I didn't know any better. But I did apologize for being that way.

That must have been hard, I said.

Well, the Lord did this for a purpose, Tito said. *So that is OK. I have a lot of pain, but it's . . . it is not for me to ask why.*

Tito slid his shoes forward in the dirt, maneuvering himself over to a rolling walker by the front door. He turned it around until the seat was close and bent his knees enough to sit.

Nana was always praying, I said. *I remember how they used to take us to the Garden of Gethsemane when Ricky and I were little. You know, there by the river? The one with the life-size statues of Jesus and Mary and the last supper?*

Oh yeah, I know it.

Nana told us that the man who made those statues, the sculptor, he was in some kind of trouble, like wounded in a battle or something during one of the world wars. She said he prayed and asked God to spare his life, to get him through the battle, and he promised God that if he lived, he'd spend the rest of his life making those statues. I remember we used to walk through there. I remember Nana praying. I think she was praying for you.

I'm just glad I never had to have a wheelchair. I was very fortunate. I could even enjoy dancing. I knew all the good nightclubs when I was young too.

Oh wow!

I loved it. I even went during the week when I was working at my photo shop down there on Congress. My feet felt like they were floating above the ground. Boy, I'll never forget that. Dancing to rock and roll music. He laughed like a fountain. *I'll never forget that.*

Apophenia

Still on my search to understand the man sleeping under the saguaro, I walk into the Tucson Museum of Art Research Library around the corner from the Molino. There are books resting on shelves or opened on large tables, reading lamps and chairs enough for a dozen people, but no one else is there besides a group of elderly women moving slowly around the room.

One of the ladies is behind a desk and alerts the others when I walk into the room. *We have a customer!* she sings.

I make a confused face in her direction. I'm not here to buy anything.

What can I help you with? she asks.

I tell her who I'm looking for, but it takes me a few minutes to explain who Sleepy is. She types something into a search engine on her computer.

Is this a Spanish image? she asks.

Yes, I say. *I mean no, it's not.*

She removes the word "Spain" from her search.

Huh, she says, *I suggest you start with the "pre-Columbian" section.* She walks me over to the middle of the room.

The ladies make small talk around me. I hear one say something about ageism and another complain that the internet has been slow all day. One wrinkles her face and peels stickers off a roll of wax paper. She wears a blue badge. Another stamps a sheet of paper and places it into a three-ring binder. The one that called me a customer makes sure I hear her comment to the other ladies that the library will be closing in thirty minutes. In silence, I open fat photo books of pre-Columbian art. Like a ghost hunter, I only find coincidences.

While Diego Rivera was painting an image of Sleepy in his mural on the courtyard walls of Mexico City's Ministry of Education, another artist named Rómulo Rozo was at the Académie de la Grande Chaumière in Paris conceiving the same image. Rozo referenced Auguste Rodin's famed bronze classic *The Thinker* to devise his own reflecting sculpture, a kind of Mesoamerican allegory, a product of Rozo's mestizo imagination. The sculptor claimed he wasn't interested in creating pre-Columbian representations of Indigeneity, but in Paris he had access to the pre-Columbian pieces housed in the schools and museums of Europe, "staging the ethnic." There were enough images to provide him with an aesthetic model, a way to see the spirit of Latinidad, far from home, through the eyes of an ancient maker.[*]

Just one year before Aurelio and Martina opened El Rapido in Tucson, Rómulo Rozo was back in the Americas presenting his new sculpture at the National Library of Mexico. Rozo had named his work *El Pensamiento* (Thought).

It was a small stone sculpture, standing only about twenty-four inches tall. A curved back. A head bowing under a peaked sombrero de charro. Sandaled feet on the ground. The figure in a fetal position, a protected and quiet stance, impenetrable. His body round, smooth, heavy stone.

Not everyone liked the image, and it may have been subjected to a mocking crowd. Some say that right after the unveiling of *El Pensamiento*, someone, perhaps a journalist or critic, placed a bottle of tequila in front of the sculpture. Then the cameras snapped, and as fast as 1932 would allow, the image went viral. Some say it was a man named Luis Alvarado who sold wooden copies of the sculpture with the bottle, transforming *El Pensamiento* into a

---

[*] Ana María Gómez Londoño, "Sueños de una tarde dominical . . . ¿Ecos de México en el arte colombiano? Tras las huellas de Diego Rivera y Rómulo Rozo" (PhD diss., Freie Universität Berlin, 2009).

popular "El Borrachito" for a fortune.* Either way, the plagiarized sculpture showed up everywhere; the reproductions of the sleeping man, usually wrapped in a blanket and topped with a wide-brimmed hat, spread throughout the country. Soon the world was introduced to an appropriated thought, an imposter, a forgery: the "Sleepy Mexican," "Pancho," or "El Borracho."

Rozo couldn't do anything about all the copies of his work, and he couldn't stop them from marketing México with his *Pensamiento*, to a stomach-churning degree. The image was plagiarized again and again until finally, the little sleeping man was hardly a thought at all—just a picture of ridicule, disgrace, and stigma for some, a clichéd curio for the rest. He became ceramic salt and pepper shakers or doorstops. A companion to the garden gnome, decorative howling coyote, and Kokopelli bookends. He was hung up or nailed down, left on a dusty shelf and forgotten.

I'm not sure who is to blame. I wonder if Rozo felt a bit of conviction, a realization that he was the one who had created an American monster. Perhaps his longing for an image to capture where we come from was nothing more than a warped dream, an Indigenous figure with no face—a person he never knew, so could never imagine honestly. In my longing, I imagine a link between Rozo and me. He's not from Tucson. He's not even Mexican. But I explore any parallel, any synchronal pattern that brings us together. Anything to make me feel like this search is not in vain. Can I tell you something? Rozo's first wife's name? It was Ana, like my mother's name. And his beloved mother's name? It was Antonia, like my dad. He even named his boy Antonio, and his daughter, Antonia. We both named one of our children by the same name. Can you imagine?

---

* Rodrigo Gutiérrez Viñuales, "Rómulo Rozo mexicanizado: Contextos y concreciones para una trayectoria (1931–1943)," in Rómulo Rozo, ¿una vanguardia propia?, ed. Christian Padilla Peñuela (Bogotá: Proyecto Bachué, 2019), 143–90.

They say Rómulo Rozo died in México, impoverished, under layers of mail sack blankets painted red, white, and green. He died in 1964, the same year my tata was written about in the newspaper, just after a successful deer season, a story about the size and weight of deers brought in by Tucson hunters that year. The reporter wrote that Tata's deer was a big one—a hefty, 105.5-pound whitetail. The man who recorded the deer's weight? His name was Tony too.

Thinking

I sat with Rodin
in a bronze mess in 1901
and with others,
los Magaña, Alvarado, y Lucero,
metal, stone, wood,
and Poet.

My Rozo
hung his head
next to stones
Thinking
thoughts of

a blasphemed image
the drinking
the eating.
My sons and daughters,
you know what gravity feels like,
to be pressed down.

Think
and feel this:
You are made
in my image. In me
you live
and move and have
your being.

Know
you are my double
bubble face in river glass. You are
my carved thoughts of longing.

—*El Pensamiento*

Clouds

I've been praying, you know. I pray every day. And this last week, man! I was so lucky. I played one machine at the casino and got it on the first bet. One hundred and forty-seven dollars! Then when I went to that old-timers' meeting with the people from Menlo, you know what happened? My first time walking in there and I won the raffle just like that. My father snaps his fingers and smiles. *Fifty bucks. Every day I pray. I been winning so much. I've been looking at the clouds, you know, and I see a lot of things.*

My father, Mr. Rapido, Tony Peyron has two nice, crisp twenty-dollar bills in his pocket. He drives a broken truck and never goes to the dentist, but most days you'll find him at a swap meet, at the dollar store, or digging through a dumpster, full to the brim with treasures that everyone else throws away. He says he is lucky, which is something close to blessed. Like being beloved. Lucky is like a voice from the clouds. It is the word my father uses to describe that incredible thing that happens when you pay attention to the gifts you are given, even the ones that don't look like much. *Open your eyeballs*, he says, his heavy hand on my head urging me to look up. Open, reach, touch, and see that sombrero-lifted, flesh and blood, that picture of rest and resolve in the clouds, that forever face to face.

Dear Pensa

Can I call you Pensa?

Can I call you mine?

How does God dance?

How do you dance?

Like I'm not ugly.
Like a bird from a cage, a color
like cream. Smelling like you,
ajo and oregano, the still
sound of your voice, of you
and in you. Your likeness

your blood like lava,
a deep pool of skin,
and legs like thick crimson rope.

Will I ever see you dance?

You will see me
like David. You will find me
in the ballrooms, in the wedding hall,
horns blasting my ballads.
Mijita, cariño, my apple,
vamos a tirar chancla,
vamos a bailar.

PART VII

Dream of a Sunday Afternoon

When I drive by the Molino now, I remember the smell of a garage kitchen and the itch of silk corn husk. I look back to the relief of standing before open freezer doors in the summertime. I remember the taste of my father's tamales—a communion of corn, the color of its skin. I remember the inside of a place I tried to run away from for so long. I remember the molino, that grinder of ideation, our processing through it, our freedom and love laid out in little wrapped-up plates of a poor man's lunch. I remember to sit and be still. On Sunday afternoon, I will eat and talk with my mother, my father, and Ricky. My corn sister knows. I will look to God and pray, like pilgrims do, for the rest to come quickly.

FIGURE 12 El Rapido's storefront mural of El Pensamiento as painted by Al "Tito" Peyron. Photo (2024) from author's personal collection.

Epilogue

May 25, 2019, was the last time I walked the halls of the Molino house. I wanted my father to cook and serve tamales one more time there so that I could tell some stories over his food. I asked for permission to use the house from the Airbnb vendor managing it. We invited some family and friends as guests, and we crammed in a few rented tables and chairs in the zaguan, in the beauty shop, in the bedrooms, and in the west room that was the first El Rapido storefront.

My father made tamales. I cooked the beans. My mother made cinnamon tea and horchata. Ricky wore a dress shirt. We had our last supper there.

It is hard to say what I felt. It was like a vapor, but not from the kitchen. Like a buzz, but not from the garden. The floors creaked, like always, and the sounds of people chattering bounced a little off the mud-brick walls, making every room vibrate in a way I had been too young to have ever witnessed before. The sunset entered the storefront window as we all ate green corn and red chile tamales. People remembered things, but their memories and stories were spoken quietly and not to me. Everyone talked about tamales and the taste of things and the best of things. Tony Peyron got some glory, but I recognized he was tired. He was happy, and also ready to go home. I thought he would be his old self at the Molino, catering and boisterous, but I suppose even Mr. Rapido changes and slows down. I can't help but feel I didn't pay close enough attention. I didn't have enough eyes and ears and tongues to be there the way I wanted to be. I wish I was big enough to witness all of it. There were many thoughts in my head, so most everything was a blur.

After the supper and stories and after everyone left, I spent the night in the house. I was afraid of being alone with the ghosts, so my mother said she would stay with me.

When the lights were off, we could hear the Saturday night people and movement in downtown Tucson. Under the watch of Sentinel Peak and before Sonoran summer sky, the slowgoing cars and trucks on Congress blasted their car stereos and the music pressed against dry air. Outside there was lots of life, but in the house, it was quiet.

Of course, the molino was not there. Only bedroom furniture and millennial chucherías filled the spaces around me. The Molino's main kitchen had been knocked down and turned into a tiny backyard with mosaic glass decor. There was no longer any space for a grinder.

Lying in bed, I had half expected something to happen—an apparition to appear in the dead of night, a hand on my shoulder, or an impression at the foot of the bed. I wondered about a visit from Aurelio and Martina. I thought I might hear the piano keys mysteriously pressed down in the zaguan. I thought of my nana and tata, mostly, and what last suppers they had with their sisters and brothers. I thought of people more ancient than them too.

At the very least, I expected to dream something wild that I had never dreamed before. This was, after all, the first and perhaps last time I would ever spend the night in the house that haunted my imagination. But in the morning I found that nothing had happened. I opened my eyes, realizing there were no phantasms. There were no sudden thuds or crash-bangs coming from the next room. There was only the sound of breath, the sound of sleeping next to my mother; together we breathed in the cold air coming from newly installed air conditioning. We breathed out, and there was no dreaming. There was only rest.

About the Author

Melani "Mele" Martinez is a senior lecturer at the University of Arizona, where she teaches writing courses. She earned a BA in creative writing at the University of Arizona and an MFA in creative nonfiction from Goucher College. Her work has appeared in *Fourth Genre, Bacopa Literary Review, Borderlore, Bearings Online, Telling Tongues: A Latin@ Anthology on Language Experience,* and *Contemporary Chicanx Writers Anthology.*